A Pictorial History of the
SCHOOL OF ENGINEERING EDUCATION
at Purdue University

David F. Radcliffe

Cataloging in Publication Data available

ISBN | 978-1-55753-771-3

CONTENTS

INTRODUCTION

This is a pictorial history of the School of Engineering Education at Purdue. Founded in 2004 by merging the Department of Freshman Engineering and the Division of Interdisciplinary Engineering Studies, this is the first academic unit of its type. This bold initiative recognized that engineering education cannot remain static if we are to address pressing global challenges such as energy, water, transportation, urbanization, health care, climate change, and sustainable food production. Tackling these challenges requires the imagination, creativity and entrepreneurial leadership of future engineers.

Purdue Engineering has a proud history of firsts in engineering education.

- First Department of Freshman Engineering (1953).
- First Honors Program at Purdue in Freshman Engineering (1958).
- First Women in Engineering Program (1969).
- Founding of National Society of Black Engineers (1975).
- Engineering Projects in Community Service (EPICS) (1995).

Drawing on this rich heritage of educational scholarship and innovation we bring a unique interdisciplinary focus on how to best engage and excite the next generation, from pre-school through high school, about the enormous opportunities for them to shape our future world as engineers; how we can increase diversity among those who do pursue engineering; and how we can transform the way new technical knowledge is created, learned and used to better society.

From its inception, Engineering Education grew and developed at a frenetic pace. A graduate program in Engineering Education was launched in 2005 and the Institute for P-12 Engineering Research and Learning (INSPIRE) was formed in 2006. A new degree in multidisciplinary engineering was developed with support from a NSF grant and submitted for ABET accreditation in 2007. Initially designated as a Department, based on these early achievements, the Board of Trustees approved the name being changed to the School of Engineering Education in 2008.

Given this rapid growth and the many changes that occurred in a short period of time it seemed important to capture the essential story of Engineering Education during these exciting formative years. Another motivation for this book was to gather up and archive a wide variety of documents, pictures and artifacts generated during this "start-up" phase. It is envisioned that these will provide a resource when a complete history of the School is written.

The mission of the School of Engineering Education is to transform engineering education based on scholarship and research. This means taking a research-based approach to the design of educational systems, similar to the way research and development drives innovation in industry. Research in engineering education provides the principles, methodologies, and educational practices upon which to build innovative curricula that educate future engineers to meet the needs of the nation and the world. This new paradigm combines deep knowledge of engineering with deep knowledge of how people learn.

This is the story of us, the people who have shaped the School of Engineering Education. This story is told through a series of chapters spanning the period 2004-2016. To establish the historical context from which the new school emerged, the opening chapter recalls its precursors, the Department of Freshman Engineering (1953-2004), and the Division of Interdisciplinary Engineering Studies (1969-2004). The concluding chapter acknowledges the many people including heads, advisory council members, outstanding alumni and alumnae, current faculty and staff and PhD graduates, who made this all possible.

Each chapter begins with a brief overview of the period covered. The evolving story is told using pictures with explanatory captions presented chronologically. The recurring theme is that of One Vision: Three Programs. A timeline thread links the images to the three programs of the School; First-Year Engineering; Interdisciplinary Engineering Studies and the Graduate Program in Engineering Education.

This pictorial timeline is augmented by a series of feature pages dispersed throughout each chapter. The purpose of these two-page spreads is to draw attention to major initiatives that are central to the unfolding story. Wherever possible, the text in the chapter openings and in the feature pages are based on quotes from contemporary documents or later accounts of activities described, drawn from authoritative sources.

This book is just a snapshot of the rich history of the School of Engineering Education; it is not intended to be a comprehensive account. Given this rich history, only a fraction of the available material could be included. Selecting which things to include from the many thousands of pictures, artifacts and articles we gathered was a daunting, near impossible task. It was simply not feasible to include everyone's favorite memory. Therefore, to complement this volume, a companion web resource is planned that will contain a more expansive collection of resources for a deeper telling of the story.

The students, staff and faculty of the School of Engineering Education deeply appreciate the generous support and sustained goodwill that so many people have provided us during this amazing journey.

We look to a promising future as we progress through our second decade, guided by our strategic vision, and encouraged by our many colleagues, friends and supporters around the world.

D Radcliffe

David F Radcliffe
Kamyar Haghighi Head
School of Engineering Education
June 2016

CHAPTER 1 FOUNDATIONS 1953–2003

The School of Engineering Education is a very young academic department, yet it has deep roots going back over half a century. A common curriculum for first-year engineering at Purdue has operated for at least 70 years and predates the Department of Freshman Engineering.

> *"In order to give the student sufficient time to adjust himself and to choose the branch of engineering for which he is best adapted, the program of study during the freshman year is common for the curricula in aeronautical engineering, air transportation, agricultural engineering, chemical engineering, civil engineering, electrical engineering, mechanical engineering, metallurgical engineering and engineering-law. Lectures and conferences will guide the student so that by the end of the second semester he may be in a position to make proper selection."*

Bulletin of Purdue University, Catalogue for 1946-1947.

Nationally, engineering education was about to undergo a fundamental transformation and Purdue played a key role under the leadership of George Hawkins who became Engineering Dean in 1953. Dean Hawkins was a member of the committee that wrote the extremely influential Report on Evaluation of Engineering Education (Grinter Report) published in 1955 and he co-led the subsequent Goals for Engineering Education report (1968) which drew heavily on the research by the staff of Freshman Engineering at Purdue. The following extract on the career of George Hawkins captures this period of momentous change.

1953 Dr. George Hawkins, Dean of Engineering, Purdue University

> *During the early years of his term as Dean of Engineering, educational programs were being impacted heavily by the information explosion that followed the release of information generated by research carried on during World War II. Assessing the importance of these developments, Dr. Hawkins was convinced that the next generation of engineers would have to be steeped in the physical and engineering sciences if they were to be able to design the complicated systems being envisioned by American industry. With imagination and courage, he took the steps required to sensitize the faculty to these developments and they, in turn, acted to achieve a major revision of the engineering curriculum at Purdue. Purdue's engineering curriculum was a model for other schools to follow-thus assisting the change to spread all across the nation.*
>
> *Dr. Hawkins worked with faculty, using faculty seminars, personal contacts, and invited scholars to challenge them to familiarize themselves with the new concepts and the new technology that was emerging. He stressed the need to be prepared for change. He also believed that contemporary engineers should have a better understanding of the social sciences and the humanities if they were to respond to society's needs and demands.*
>
> *His ideas about a dynamic and changing curriculum were challenged and resisted by some; but with patience and sincerity, he pressed his points. Younger members of the faculty rallied to his cause, and he, in turn, encouraged them to absorb themselves in the work at the scientific frontier of engineering. This they did with a sense of pride and dedication; and curricula changed to reflect an emphasis on applied science rather than the "art" of engineering. Despite his administrative responsibilities, he, himself, devoted as much time as he possibly could to remain at the research forefront of his own specialty-heat and mass transfer.*
>
> *On the national scene in the early 1960's, Dr. Hawkins was asked to be cochairman of the American Society of Engineering Education's goals study. This study was undertaken at the request of the Engineers Council for Professional Development and was financially underwritten by the National Science Foundation. Once more he made clear his beliefs in a scientifically oriented engineering curriculum, heavily bolstered by advanced graduate study. He was joined in this by many educators who contributed to this study; but again he ran into opposition from some educators across the country. However, as time went by, the view expressed in the Goals Report, was, by and large, accepted nationally.*

Hancock, J.C. (1979) George Andrew Hawkins (1907-1978), in Memorial Tributes, Vol 1, National Academies Press, pp112-117.

1956 Purdue lecture hall

1951 ↓ Foundry sand mixing laboratory

1952 ↓ Electrical engineering laboratory

[1950]

1953 —
Albert Spalding, Founding Department Head of Freshman Engineering

1952 ↓ Engineering drawing laboratory

1956 ↓ Welding class for engineering students

1954 —
Department of Freshman Engineering established

[1959]

FRESHMAN ENGINEERING

The creation of the Department of Freshman Engineering was announced in 1954.

> *A Department of Freshman Engineering has been established this year in a reorganization within the engineering schools with Dr. A. R. Spalding of the Mechanical Engineering department as its head. The educational objectives of this new department are extended academic counseling and related services, studying and planning the freshman curriculum and administering the common program carried by all freshman engineering students. Associate Dean W. A. Knapp, who has had charge of the freshman engineering program for many years, will continue to be closely associated with it until his retirement next year.*
>
> Spalding to Head Freshman Engineering, *The Purdue Alumnus* Vol XLII, No 1, Sept-Oct 1954, p16.

In the previous year, Dean Hawkins set up a faculty committee chaired by Dr. Spalding to revise this common first year curriculum.

> *The Faculty Committee on Freshman Engineering was established in December 1953, to develop and promote an effective program of preparedness and competence for freshmen"..... The purpose was to provide the students with a plan of study that will stimulate interest in their engineering career and to enable them to continue their course as upperclassmen at such level to provide the profession with the best prepared young engineers to be obtained anywhere. -G, A. Hawkins, Dean of Engineering.*
>
> Trowbride, R. (1995) Prof. Spaulding Answers Your Questions About the Changes, *The Purdue Engineer*, December, pp14-15, 29.

December 1953 ↑ *"This committee formulated the recently adopted freshman engineering program. Faculty members of every engineering school are represented in this group."*

Front Row, Left to Right: Warren E. Howland, C.E., Frederick J. Bogardus, M.E., William K. LeBold, Engineering, Educational Reference; John B. Liljedahl, Ag. E., Stephen B. Elrod, C.E., Gerald W. Issacs, Ag.E.

Back Row, Left to Right: A. R. Holowenko, M.E., J. B. Jones, M.E., J. L. Waling, C.E., E. O. Stitz, E.Sc., A. R. Spaulding, Dean of Freshman Engineering, S. C. Hite, Chem. E., M. E. Shanks, A.E., C. T. Marek, Met.E., S. L. Shaw, Office of Admissions. Not shown are the following: Stephen Freeman, E.E., H. W. White, Office of Admissions.

Trowbride, R. (1995) Prof. Spaulding Answers Your Questions About the Changes, The Purdue Engineer, December, pp14-15, 29.

December 1953 *"Here Professor Spaulding explains the new curriculum to Boyd Christensen, a senior at West Lafayette High School who plans to enter Purdue next fall. Looking on is Mr. Cari M. Hammer, principal of West Lafayette High School. The up-graded curriculum is expected to make a good selling point for Purdue's engineering schools."*

Trowbride, R. (1995) Prof. Spaulding Answers Your Questions About the Changes, The Purdue Engineer, December, pp14-15, 29.

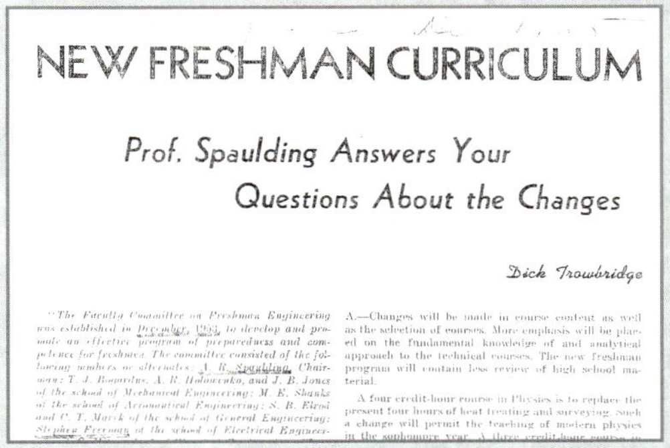

NEW FRESHMAN CURRICULUM

Prof. Spaulding Answers Your Questions About the Changes

Dick Trowbridge

"*The Faculty Committee on Freshman Engineering was established in December, 1953, to develop and promote an effective program of preparedness and competence for freshmen. The committee consisted of the following members or alternates: A. R. Spaulding, Chairman; T. J. Bogardus, A. R. Holowenko, and J. B. Jones of the school of Mechanical Engineering; M. E. Shanks of the school of Aeronautical Engineering; S. B. Elrod and C. T. March of the school of General Engineering; Stephen Freeman of the school of Electrical Engineer-*

A.—Changes will be made in course content as well as the selection of courses. More emphasis will be placed on the fundamental knowledge of and analytical approach to the technical courses. The new freshman program will contain less review of high school material.

A four credit-hour course in Physics is to replace the present four hours of heat treating and surveying. Such a change will permit the teaching of modern physics in the sophomore year. A three credit-hour course in

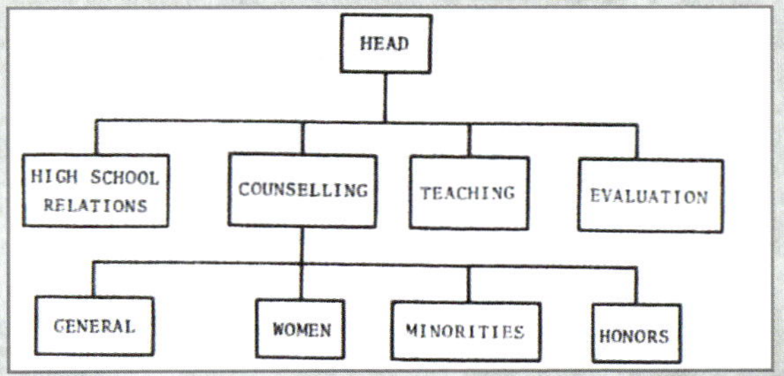

November 1978 ***"Figure 1*** *Functional Diagram of the Department of Freshman Engineering"*

By 1978, the operations of Freshman Engineering had diversified somewhat.

> *There is an honors program for students who are well prepared in high school, a counselor tutorial program for students who are academically disadvantaged, programs to consider the special needs of women and minorities, and a general program for the many students who are classified as regular or average students. As shown in Figure 1, Freshman Engineering has a high school relations program and teaches some freshman courses.*
>
> *The counseling functions of the department include orientation, placement and academic advising. Orientation refers to contacts with the student prior to registration: placement refers to the selection of beginning freshman courses and academic advising refers to counselling directed primarily to academic areas.*
>
> *In addition to the individual counselling that is available throughout the year, there is group counselling in the form of a one hour course, Engineering 100, Freshman Engineering Lectures. Each week the heads of the various Schools of Engineering or their representatives meet with the students and discuss their engineering programs. They usually discuss their curricula, job opportunities, where their students are employed after graduation and specifically what engineers in their field are doing. Salary and future outlook are also discussed. These lectures usually terminate with a question and answer period.*
>
> Butler, B.R. McDowell, R.W and LeBold, W.K (1978) Purdue Freshman Engineering Orientation, Placement, Counselling and Evaluation, *ERM*.Vol11 Issue: 1, pp 5-10, 29.

1966 ↓ Professor Bill LeBold visiting with students in the student lounge

[1960]

1966 ↓ Engineering Design Project *Magnitrain*

1968 ↑ Based on extensive data analysis, the Goals Report presents the direction which engineering education, graduate and undergraduate, must take if it is to meet the demands of the future.

1967 —
Clifford Gerde named
Department Head of Freshman Engineering

1969 —
Division of Interdisciplinary Engineering Studies established;
Richard Grace named Founding Head

[1969]

RESEARCH AND INNOVATION

Educational research was a vital part of the Department of Freshman Engineering from the 1960s.

> *Since the first FIE conference a quarter of a century ago, our engineering educational research at Purdue has shifted from status-quo oriented research to action-oriented research. Earlier our emphasis was on providing information, examining relationships, identifying strengths and delineating problems. We analyzed the correlation of high school grades and test scores with college GPA. We documented trends in enrollment, grades, and retention. We surveyed students and graduates regarding the quality and relevance of their education. Sometimes we even defined areas requiring action.*
>
> *However, after the first FIE Conference 25 years ago, our research efforts shifted to action-oriented research. How could we use educational research information to change and improve engineering education? In this paper we will describe action-oriented research that has significantly improved placement in beginning courses, helped students make more informed career decisions, increased and retained more women and minority students, and enhanced our programs for honors and higher risk students. We will also describe how we have extended our educational research efforts beyond our own campus and are sharing our educational research findings and action-oriented programs with other institutional settings and colleagues all over the world. And lastly, we will speculate on what direction institutional and collaborative engineering educational research is likely to take during the next quarter of a century.*

LeBold, W.K and Ward, S. K. (1995) 25 Years of Frontiers Educational Research: The Call for Action-Oriented Research, *Proceedings Frontiers in Education*, Atlanta.

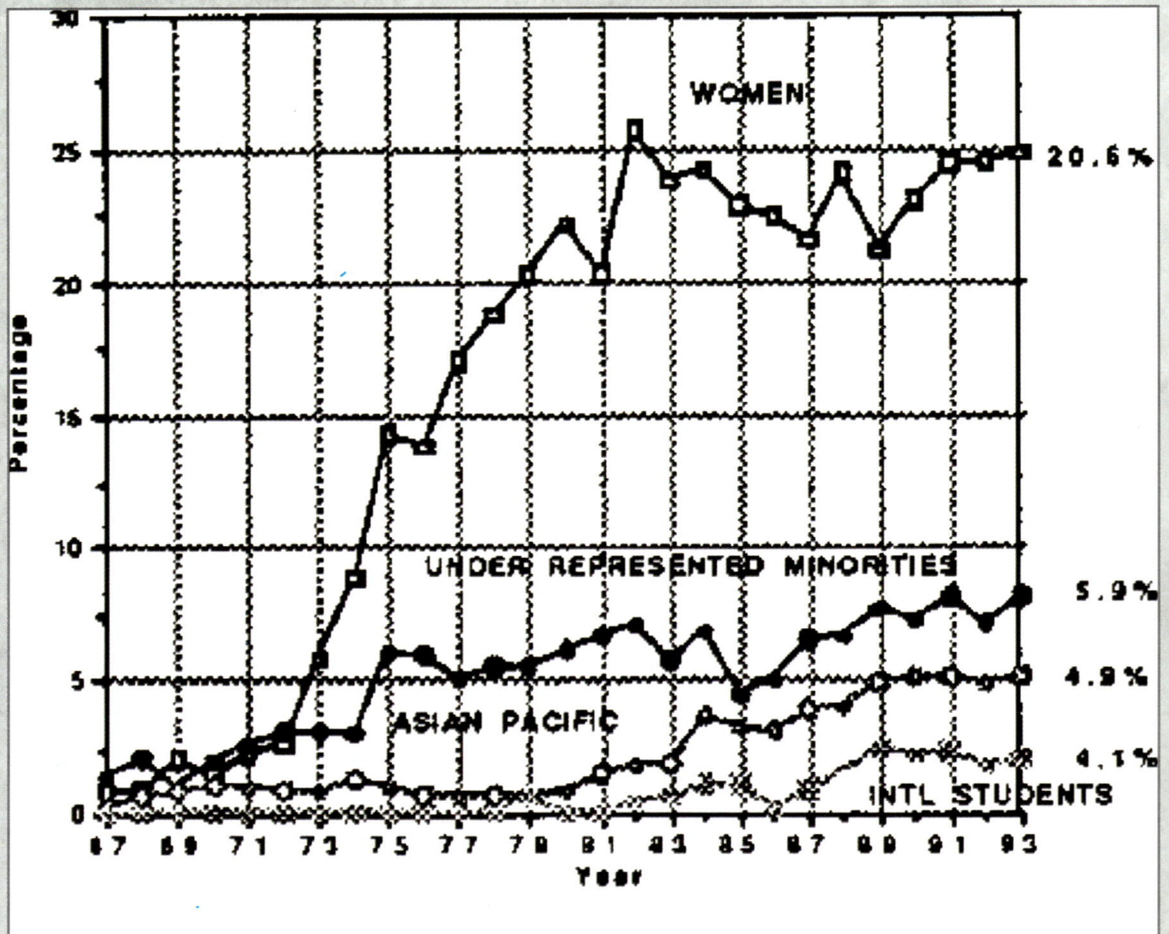

Figure 1: Diversity Trends Among Purdue Beginning Engineering Students

1995 ↑ The figure represents diversity trends among Purdue first year engineering students between the years 1967 - 1993 as reported in the 1995 FIE Conference paper

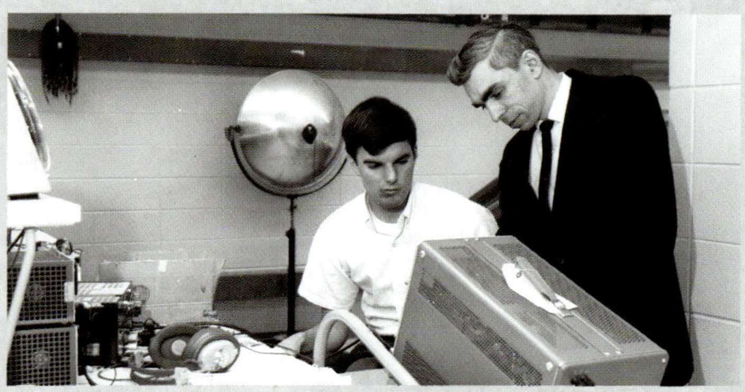

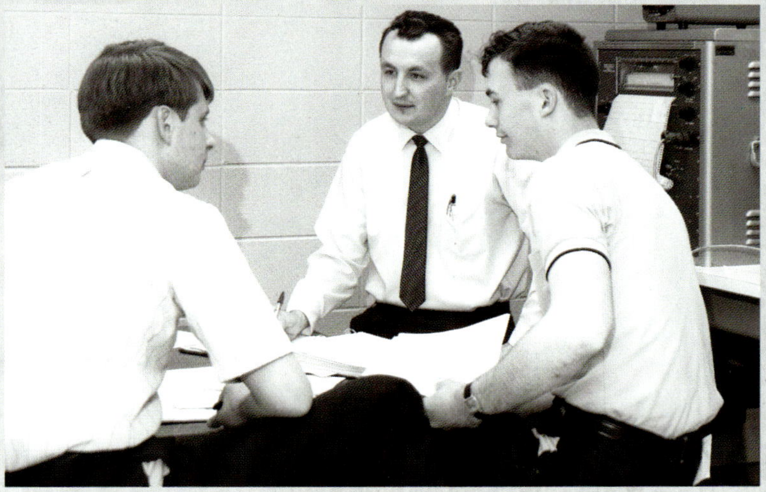

1969 ↓↑ Photos showcase Professor Lindenlaub and students exercising ATI techniques

Top Left: *"Students learn the functions of the controls of a spectrum analyzer. Audio instruction allows them to see, touch, and operate the instrument while listening to the tape."*

Top Right: *"The author (right) discusses an extension of an experiment with a student. Since the student is not forced to proceed quickly, any topic which he finds especially interesting can be explored to any depth he desires."*

Bottom Left: *"An oral examination session provides an opportunity for a face to face discussion between a Graduate Instructor and students."*

Lindenlaub, J. (1969) Applying Audio Tutorial Techniques to Laboratory Instruction. *IEEE Transactions on Education*, Vol. E-12, No. 2.

1993 ↑ *Teaching Engineering* co-authored by Purdue University Professors Phillip Wankat and Frank Oreovicz

In 1967, Professor John Lindenlaub (EE) adapted audio tutorial instruction (ATI) techniques in his laboratory on Information Transmission, Modulation and Noise, a senior course in communications theory. The idea of audio tutorials came from Professor Sam Postlethwait in biology at Purdue. Originally conceived as a system of supplementary instruction for weaker freshmen, ATI became a method for supporting independent study for any student. It was an early form of "flipping the lecture."

Based on the growing reputation for instructional innovation at Purdue, the NSF-funded a Center for Instructional Development in Engineering (CIDE) from 1977-1983 headed by John Lindenlaub. The CIDE hired Dr. Frank Oreovicz as a communications specialist and they ran faculty workshops, a luncheon seminar series plus a summer faculty development program. CIDE facilities included a place for course materials development enabling faculty to produce rapid results. Inspired by his experience of the center, Professor Phil Wankat (ChE) completed an M.S. in Education, Counseling and Personnel Services in 1981.

Professor Wankat teamed with Frank Oreovicz in 1983 to create and co-teach the first engineering course in the USA to prepare engineering PhD students for academic careers. It drew on knowledge about how people learn from the literature – translating this research into teaching practice. Their widely used book Teaching Engineering was first published in 1993. Their course Education Methods in Engineering is still taught today and was a foundational part of the Graduate Certificate in Engineering Education.

Based on ENE Interdisciplinary Colloquium, *Indomitable Innovators,* November 2013.

1970 ↓ Engineering classroom in Duncan Annex

1971 ↓ Summer Engineering Conference

1971 ↓ LEFT TO RIGHT Summer Engineering Conference for Freshman Engineers

[1970]

1973 —
Harold Amrine named Department Head of Freshman Engineering

1974 ↓ Minority Engineering Program launches at Purdue

1974 ↓ Donna Frohreich, Assistant Professor and Founding Director of the Women in Engineering Program at Purdue University

1976 ↓ Women in Engineering Career Conference

1976 ↓ Dr. LeBold assisting Women in Engineering Career Conference

1977 ↓ Student Interviews in Stewart Center

[1979]

INTERDISCIPLINARY ENGINEERING STUDIES

The founding head of the program, Dr. Richard Grace, described the Interdisciplinary Engineering Studies program in these terms at the fall IEEE Electronics Conference held in Chicago in October 1971.

> *The Division of Interdisciplinary Engineering Studies at Purdue University was created in response to student, faculty, and industrial needs for engineers more broadly educated than ever before. After more than a year of planning the Trustees of Purdue University founded and the faculty of the Schools of Engineering implemented the Division in 1969-70. The founding document states:*
>
> > *"The primary responsibility of the Division will be to provide a coordinated and controlled educational opportunity for students whose interest and talents, while strongly oriented toward engineering and science, do not coincide with the presently established professional curricula in the existing Schools of Engineering."*
>
> *In addition to the traditional academic structure, a forum was needed for those faculty members who had common interests but were housed in different schools and buildings. A related need was to draw the students and faculty together and to include student views in the curriculum-making processes. Perhaps most important of all, students and faculty alike wished to experiment with certain phases of engineering education, primarily as they relate to contemporary social problems. Lastly, rather than to proliferate both the number of designated degree offerings and the number of engineering departments, the concept of a single Division of Interdisciplinary Engineering Studies emerged.*
>
> *The largest enrollment in new programs is in the fields of bioengineering, engineering management, environmental engineering, nuclear engineering, and systems engineering. Foremost in the thinking of the students is the social relevance which their studies have; the other main factor which students seek is flexibility in designing their own plan of study to meet graduation requirements for the BSE degree.*

Grace, R.E. (1971) Interdisciplinary Engineering Studies Purdue University, *Proceedings of the IEEE Fall Electronics Conference*, Chicago, October 18-20, pp83-85.

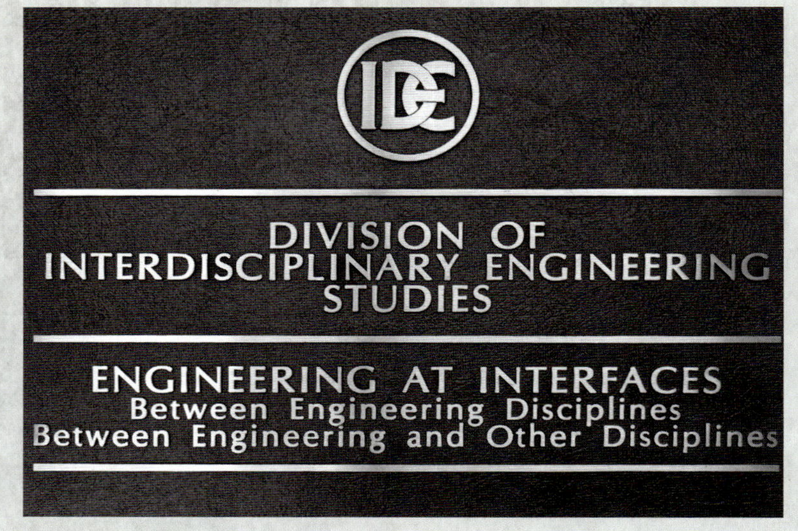

Interdisciplinary Engineering Studies wall plaque once displayed in the Engineering Administration building (ENAD)

1974 ↑ Blaine Butler and Richard McDowell advising students. IDE alumnus Bruce Clarke ('78) stated, "Dr. Butler was very influential with my career path by encouraging me to take a new class that was introducing computer engineering—first of its kind."

The Interdisciplinary Engineering Association of Students is an organization which allows IDE students to meet each other. It also keeps its members in contact with industry through plant trips and speakers.

1985 ↓ Interdisciplinary Engineering Association of Students (IDEAS)

1974 ↓ IDE student Howard Gobstein (front, second from left), VP of Purdue Student Body

Table 2. IDE Enrollment, Spring 1979.

Major Area of Study	*Number*
Acoustical Engineering	10
Applied Mathematics	4
Architectural Engineering	25
Biomedical Engineering	61
Computer Systems	12
Engineering Geology	13
Engineering Management	39
Engineering Science	12
Environmental Engineering	47
Inventive Design	4
Ocean Engineering	15
Power Engineering	8
Preprofessional	8
Systems Engineering	7
Transportation Engineering	7
Urban Studies	3
All other titles	29
Total	310

1979 ↑ IDE Enrollment for the Spring of 1979 as reported in Grace's publication, *Nontraditional Engineering Programs: The Purdue Experience, Engineering Education*

In a 1979 paper published in Engineering Education, Dr. Grace made this assessment of the first ten years of IDES program.

Interdisciplinary education at the undergraduate level is relatively new to engineering education. Experience in three developing fields recently has been reviewed in detail: environmental engineering, biomedical engineering, and engineering management.

The overriding observation at Purdue and other large institutions is that many undergraduate students are quick to seek and accept new educational endeavors in engineering. In most disciplinary programs, the new is threaded into existing courses, new electives, new departmental specialties at the graduate level-all in the name of depth. Those students who enter interdisciplinary, nontraditional fields of engineering sacrifice depth in one discipline for additional breadth gained by study in two or more fields, not necessarily even engineering.

An external constraint faced by graduates of nontraditional engineering programs is that they are often not accredited by ECPD. While this poses few problems for those entering industry, graduates who seek careers that involve public works or public funding frequently face completion of the EIT as a requisite for employment.

Finally, the marketplace has been receptive to the nontraditional engineering graduate. Companies that visit Purdue have learned of the availability of nontraditional engineering graduates and quickly polarize into two camps-the receptive and non-receptive. Non-receptive companies are commonly in the aerospace and chemical industries, which normally visit the University to find a fairly specific type of graduate. On the other hand, the automotive industries represent one example where nontraditional opportunities in engineering appear to abound. .... As this view diffuses throughout American industry, and as new companies are formed for activities not yet dreamed of, the role of the nontraditional engineering graduate-often the generalist- is sure to continue to be an important one.

Grace, R.E (1979) Nontraditional Engineering Programs: The Purdue Experience, *Engineering Education*, Vol 70, December, p 261.

1996 ⇣ Freshman Engineering Computer Class

2001 ⇣ Jane Daniels, Director of the Women in Engineering Program (1980-2011) advising student

[1980]

1981 —
Richard Grace named Department Head of Freshman Engineering

1982 —
David Kessler named IDES Head

1987 —
Phillip Wankat named Department Head of Freshman Engineering

1996 —
Victor Goldschmidt named Department Head of Freshman Engineering

1999 —
Gregory Ayers
Outstanding Alumni Award

2002 ↓ Department of Freshman Engineering

2000 —
Jennifer Sinclair Curtis named Department Head of Freshman Engineering and **Phillip Wankat** named IDES Head
2003 —
Kamyar Haghighi named Department Head of Freshman Engineering

2001 —
Paul Cloyd, Sue Hudson-Abreu
Outstanding Alumni Award
2002 —
Michael Cave, David Schwind
Outstanding Alumni Award
2003 —
Geoffrey Crowley
Outstanding Alumni Award

[2003]

CHAPTER 2 VISION 2004–2007

Recognizing the need for reform in engineering education, highlighted in numerous reports from the mid-1990s onwards, Purdue Engineering set forth a bold vision to create a first-of-its-type School of Engineering Education. This vision is encapsulated in the executive summary of a report entitled Toward the Future, *Engineering Education at Purdue: A Vision for Preeminence*, issued in January 2004.

> *Schools of Engineering propose a vision for preeminence in engineering education through a bold new initiative that may serve as the first step to drastically improve engineering education in the United States. This plan will legitimize, institutionalize, and advance preeminent programs in engineering education by establishing a School of Engineering Education. If accepted, this plan will propel Purdue University and the Schools of Engineering to the forefront as a national leader in engineering education.*
>
> *Schools of Engineering propose a vision for preeminence in engineering education through a bold new initiative that may serve as the first step to drastically improve engineering education in the United States. This plan will legitimize, institutionalize, and advance preeminent programs in engineering education by establishing a School of Engineering Education. If accepted, this plan will propel Purdue University and the Schools of Engineering to the forefront as a national leader in engineering education.*
>
> *Through this vision and plan, we seek to:*
>
> - *Elevate the first-year engineering program to preeminence through development of innovative classroom experiences and partnerships.*
> - *Bring the administration of the non-accredited undergraduate Interdisciplinary Engineering program under the School of Engineering Education and create a new accredited undergraduate interdisciplinary engineering program.*
> - *Create a new undergraduate Engineering Education program through Interdisciplinary Engineering (IDE).*
> - *Establish a coherent research agenda focused on student learning and learning environments. This research and discovery base will support systemic reform of engineering education.*
> - *Create new graduate degree programs (MS and PhD) to support the research agenda and prepare the next generation of professionals to impact engineering education reform.*
> - *Develop a structured outreach program to engage K-12 audiences in engineering, enhance recruitment efforts for the Schools of Engineering, and develop networks of faculty to pursue research center proposals.*
> - *Establish an engaged partnership with industry to provide feedback to evaluate the quality of students and our educational programs.*
>
> *Purdue has the unique opportunity to redefine engineering education and lead the nation in educational preeminence. The mission of the new School of Engineering Education (SEED) will advance the successful components of the existing Department of Freshman Engineering and recognize the opportunities in taking a leadership role in engineering education reform. This vision and plan is also in line not only with the strategic plan goals of the Schools of Engineering and Purdue University but also with the investment Purdue has made in the educational and outreach components of the Discovery Park and other research centers .*

On April 9, 2004, the Purdue Board of Trustees approved the formation of the Department of Engineering Education.

> *Trustee Essex brought forth a request to consolidate the Department of Freshman Engineering and the Division of Interdisciplinary Engineering Studies to form a new department named the Department of Engineering Education. This will allow Purdue to make a better presentation in the K-12 arena, provide more opportunities for the students in these current disciplines, and will permit full accreditation in the Department of Engineering Education. Committee Chairman Essex staled that a lengthy discussion and presentation was given at the committee meeting yesterday.*

The Board approved a name change to the School of Engineering Education in February 2008.

2005 Kamyar Haghighi

↓ Freshman Engineering working late into the evening in the Engineering Administration Building (ENAD)

↓ Freshman Engineering Design Project

[2004]

January — *"Towards the Future"* recommends a School of Engineering of Engineering Education (SEED)

Deborah Follman
CoE Dean A.A. Potter Faculty Award of Excellence

Andrea Turcatti
CoE Leadership Award

Robert Montgomery
CoE Advising Award

Debra Felix
CoE Customer Service Award

↓ Freshman Engineering Computer Lab

April — Board of Trustees approved creation of Department of Engineering Education

[2004]

↓↑ Planning the Department of Engineering Education in May | Includes (top left) Phil Wankat, PK Imbrie, John Gaunt, (lower left) Richard Lesh, Neal Houze, John Lindenlaub, Bob Montgomery, William Oakes, (lower right) Heidi Diefes-Dux, Mike Harris, George Bodner

[2004]

↓ Billi Jennings advising a first-year engineering student

↓ Bill LeBold reviewing research

[2004]

RESEARCH AGENDA

Between September 2005 and February 2006 three meetings were held to synthesize a national research agenda for engineering education in the US. A report on these National Engineering Education Research Colloquies was published in the *Journal of Engineering Education* in October 2006 summarizing this initiative.

Will the U.S. have engineers prepared to collaborate and lead in a rapidly changing world? The answer to that question, in part, relies on our ability to transform how we educate our future engineers. Our premise is that we need fundamental knowledge of how engineers learn to under-gird these transformational decisions. With support from the National Science Foundation, the Engineering Education Research Colloquies (EERC) were designed to collaboratively develop a national research framework and agenda to conduct rigorous engineering education research. The endeavor represents the collective effort of more than seventy engineering, science, and mathematics education researchers, learning scientists, and practitioners who worked together during three face-to-face meetings.

Participants in Colloquy One used a reverse roadmap process with progressive refinement to identify major engineering education research themes. The process used in excess of fifty-five desirable outcomes (i.e., competencies and attributes) of a graduating engineer as the discussion starting point. Three categories of outcomes were identified: established outcomes (those that are defined by ABET EC2000 and have already been widely discussed in the engineering education community, e.g., teamwork, communication skills); emerging outcomes (those that are newly identified in the literature and are currently part of the national debate, e.g., the nature of innovation, practical ingenuity); and opportunity outcomes (future outcomes that are being discussed locally or will be required to advance the future of engineering education, e.g., understanding globalization and its impact on the workforce, dealing with setbacks and failure).

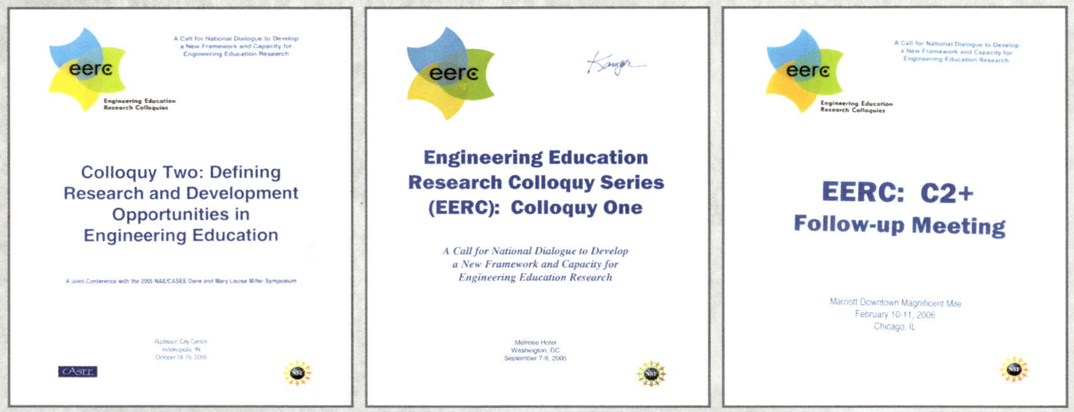

2005-2006 ↓ Title pages for the three Engineering Education Research Colloquies

2006 ↓ Gary Gabriele, Sue Kemnitzer, Kamyar Haghighi and Karen Watson at EERC meeting

Special Report

The Research Agenda for the New Discipline of Engineering Education

I. INTRODUCTION

Rapid changes in the worldwide engineering enterprise are creating a compelling rationale for us to rethink how we should educate future generations of engineers [1–4]. According to *The Engi-*

stage and position us to begin addressing national and global grand challenges.

The Engineering Education Research Colloquies (EERC) were designed with this transformational change in mind [9]. Representing a collaborative effort of more than 70 engineering, sci-

2006 ↓ Description of the research agenda

Research Agenda for the New Discipline of Engineering Education

Area 1—Engineering Epistemologies: Research on what constitutes engineering thinking and knowledge within social contexts now and into the future.

Area 2—Engineering Learning Mechanisms: Research on engineering learners' developing knowledge and competencies in context.

Area 3—Engineering Learning Systems: Research on the instructional culture, institutional infrastructure, and epistemology of engineering educators.

Area 4—Engineering Diversity and Inclusiveness: Research on how diverse human talents contribute solutions to the social and global challenges and relevance of our profession.

Area 5—Engineering Assessment: Research on, and the development of, assessment methods, instruments, and metrics to inform engineering education practice and learning.

Special Report (2006) The Research Agenda for the New Discipline of Engineering Education, *Journal of Engineering Education*, 95(4), pp 259-61.

2006 ↓ Summary of the five research areas

The list of engineering education research themes developed during Colloquy One served as the starting point for the next colloquy. Participants in Colloquy Two used a COGS (Challenges, Opportunities, Gaps, and Strengths) analysis to transform the research themes into nineteen explicit research clusters. These nineteen research clusters were then synthesized during a third EERC meeting.

The resultant five priority research areas were Engineering Epistemologies, Engineering Learning Mechanisms, Engineering Learning Systems, Engineering Diversity and Inclusiveness, and Engineering Assessment.

We believe these research areas will ensure a coherent, rigorous and innovative foundation for systemic and sustained transformation of our engineering education system. Thus, better preparing our graduates to adapt to the rapidly evolving technical, social, and global environment and to be leaders in addressing societal challenges.

Faculty from the new Department of Engineering Education played a leading role in the creation of this national research agenda. The members of the steering committee for the national EERC Colloquies were *Robin Adams, Norman Fortenberry, Kamyar Haghighi, PK Imbrie, Leah Jamieson, Jack Lohmann, Teri Reed-Rhoads, and Karl Smith.*

↓ LEFT TO RIGHT | William Oakes, Bill LeBold, PK Imbrie, John Gaunt, George Bodner, Sean Brophy

↓ Karl Smith and Dale Harris

[2005]

ABOUT THIS SPREAD *First Engineering Education Research Advance at the West Lafayette, Indiana Holiday Inn in May.* *Learn more about Advance on page 46.*

⇣ Kamyar Haghighi

⇣ Monica Cox and Demetra Evangelou

February — ICHE approves Graduate Program

Robin Adams, Sean Brophy, Monica Cox, Karl Smith
New Faculty Members

[2005]

Breaking ground on the Millennium Building (Neil Armstrong Hall of Engineering)

Promoting Engineering Education at the GCEE 2005, Sydney

Deborah Follman advising first-year engineering students in the Engineering Administration building, formerly known as ENAD

[2005]

August —ENE Graduate Program begins

↓ EPICS student project principles of colored light demonstration

↓ Bob Montgomery teaching first-year engineering students

↓ Co-founders of EPICS (Engineering Projects in Community Service)—William Oakes , Leah Jamieson and Edward Coyle—awarded the 2005 Bernard M. Gordon Prize for Innovation in Engineering and Technology Education by the National Academy of Engineering

William Oakes
National Academy of Engineering
Gordon Prize Recipient

Katie Boyce, John Gaunt,
P.K. Imbrie, William Oakes
CoE Team Award: First-Year Honors Program

Phillip Wankat
CoE Mentoring Award

[2005]

GRADUATE PROGRAM

Getting the graduate program operational as soon as humanly possible was an urgent priority for the founding faculty. They managed to design the program, get it approved by all the relevant authorities including the Indiana Commission for Higher Education by February 2005 and have it operational later that year. They envisaged two MS degrees; one for people with a BS in a technical field other than engineering and one for those with a BS in engineering. Students would enroll either directly into the PhD program or after completing an MS.

This degree program will be designed to prepare the recipient for a career in engineering education at the undergraduate or post-graduate level. Students with expertise in qualitative and quantitative research methods will be well-positioned to work for K-12 schools, community colleges, and universities as well as other nonprofit and for-profit organizations (including testing organizations, foundations, governmental organizations, etc.) as faculty members, researchers, assessment and accreditation coordinators, policy makers, program officers, curriculum designers, corporate trainers, and directors of teaching/learning centers, diversity programs, or outreach programs.

M.S. degree programs will provide students with an understanding of engineering principles and applications and the pedagogical techniques required to teach engineering principles and applications. The master's programs will be designed for students who are interested in pursuing careers in community college or K-12 education (including teachers or math/science coordinators for school districts) or in obtaining doctorate degrees in engineering education. Students pursuing master's degrees may also be interested in careers in corporate training.

To obtain a Ph.D. in engineering education, students must i) complete 36-48 course credit hours beyond those achieved for the bachelor's degree, ii) pass a cumulative exam in a traditional engineering content area, iii) write and defend an original

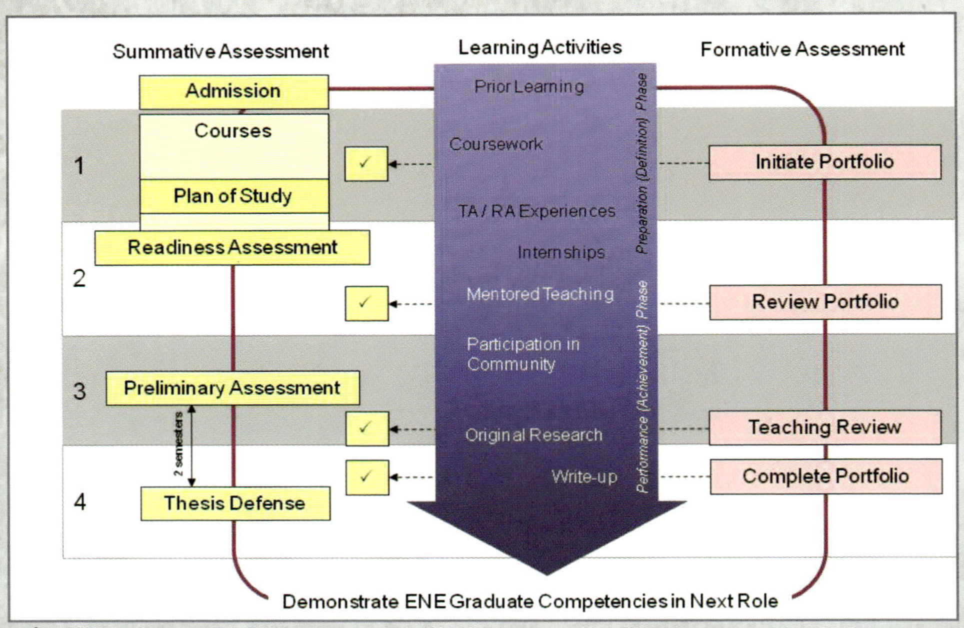

PhD Roadmap approved in November 2007

Graduate class in the early days of the program

Approved: 10/05/2005

PURDUE UNIVERSITY - ENGINEERING EDUCATION
Graduate Competencies

Engineering Education Graduate Competencies

The aim of the graduate competencies is to help each student develop the ability to create and synthesize knowledge; think critically and reflectively; master written and oral communication skills; demonstrate engineering skills, engage in professional development; participate actively in professional field or engineering education; teaching engineering, and apply their knowledge of instruction, curriculum design, and assessment of engineering science, problem-solving, and design appropriately. Opportunities for developing materials to demonstrate competencies will occur in coursework and other settings. Competencies gained through prior education and/or experience can also be applied to the requirements, with appropriate documentation in the portfolio.

1. **Synthesize Knowledge** The graduate will read and synthesize educational literature, describe fundamental theories of human learning, and apply knowledge of human learning, diversity, and effective pedagogy to the solution of practical problems in his/her discipline. Students will demonstrate achievement of one or more of the following to satisfy this competency.
   - Write a critical literature review
   - Write a conference paper based on the standards of either a state, regional or national conference
   - Write a grant proposal based on published grant guidelines
   - Write a journal article based on the publication guidelines for a national or comparable journal
   - Write a project report based on a research project
   - Design and implement an instructional development project
   - Actively participate in the design and implementation of a course or a workshop and write a critical report
2. **Create Knowledge** The graduate will describe common research methods in his/her discipline, read and evaluate educational research, and apply research findings to the solution of practical problems in his/her discipline. Students will demonstrate achievement of one or more of the following to satisfy this competency.
   - Conduct a mini-research project individually or collaboratively with peers or faculty
   - Conduct engineering education research
   - Develop instructional materials based on research findings and/or theory
3. **Communicate Knowledge** The graduate will communicate effectively in both oral and written formats including the ability to communicate content from his/her discipline through the design and delivery of effective teaching/learning activities that integrate content and pedagogy, adapt instruction and support services to the needs of diverse learners, and appropriately assess learning outcomes. All of this is to be demonstrated using inclusive and non-biased language in both written and oral communication. Students will demonstrate achievement in an appropriate combination of activities from the following list to satisfy this competency.
   - Present at one university, state, regional, or national meeting, class or colloquium
   - Present the results of an independent study project at the Seminar in Engineering Education
   - Submit an article to an appropriate journal
   - Explain problem solutions (i.e. serve as a TA for an engineering course)
   - Develop instructional materials that communicate information to diverse end users
4. **Think Critically and Reflectively** The graduate will develop a personal vision of inclusive educational practice, identify the relationship of his/her discipline to the broader field of education, and critically evaluate theory and practice. Students will demonstrate achievement of one or more of the following to satisfy this competency.
   - Prepare a critical and reflective paper on scholarly topics in engineering education
   - Prepare a constructive critique of a research design
   - Prepare a constructive critique of a current research theory in engineering education
   - Prepare a journal or reflective piece on one's growth in understanding of what it means to be a teacher (i.e. for an engineering or engineering education course)
   - Prepare a constructive critique on how to address equity and diversity issues in engineering education
   - Critique research design in engineering education

Purdue University • Engineering Education • Graduate Programs Page 3
www.purdue.edu/ENE/Graduate •

↓ The first four of ten graduate competencies for the PhD in Engineering Education

proposal for research in engineering education, and iv) conduct research for, write, and defend a Ph.D. dissertation on an engineering education topic. A master's degree is not required as part of the Ph.D. program, although credits earned in master's programs will often count towards the Ph.D. requirements.

Katehi, L.P.B., Banks, K., Diefes-Dux, H.A., Follman, D.K., Gaunt, J., Haghighi, K., Imbrie, P.K., Jamieson, L.H., Montgomery, R.E., Oakes, W.C. and Wankat, P. (2004) Development of Graduate Programs in Engineering Education, *Proceedings ASEE Annual Conference*, Salt Lake City, Session 2555.

Initially only a direct entry PhD was offered. This strategic decision was taken to ensure the rapid growth of the research base of the new school at a time when there were relatively few faculty and hence limited capacity to support both MS and PhD students. A defining characteristic of our PhD is the portfolio based on ten graduate competencies (see figure). Each graduate is challenged to create a reflective portfolio of their professional capabilities framed by these ten areas of professional performance.

An MS program was implemented in 2014 and a Graduate Certificate in Engineering Education was approved in fall 2015. The latter was aimed at PhD students in technical engineering fields at Purdue who aspired to future faculty positions and wanted to gain up-to-date knowledge of teaching and learning theory and practice and how to be successful as a professor.

During its first decade, the graduate program in engineering education graduated a total of 63 PhDs, a number that was almost unimaginable at the start. Two thirds of these are female. The vast majority of these alumni and alumnae are employed in higher education in a variety of research, instructional or administrative roles while others work with professional associations, as consultants or in industry.

↓ Faculty and staff of Engineering Education at the retirement event for John Gaunt | LEFT TO RIGHT Deb Arihood, Cathy Elwell, Larry Huggins, Jim Barany, Kamyar Haghighi, Phil Wankat, John Gault, Doug Sutton, William Oakes, David Bowker

[2006]

INSPIRE Formed
Teri Reed-Rhodes named Inaugural Director

↓ IDE student Scott Krenzke in Acoustical Engineering at the sound board

↓ Sean Brophy sharing research findings at the Summer Undergraduate Research Fellowship Program (SURF)

Demetra Evangelou, Matthew Ohland, Terri Reed-Rhoads, Ruth Streveler
New Faculty Members

Deborah Follman
NSF CAREER

[2006]

First-Year Honors students learning community designing a roller coaster

K-12 teachers engaged in summer workshop

[2006]

Margo Denner
CoE New Employee Award

William Oakes
CoE A.A. Potter Award
CoE Engagement Service Award

↓ Preparing to move out of the Engineering Administration Building

↓ Neil Armstrong Hall of Engineering construction progression

First PhD Graduate
Tamara Moore

[2006]

INSPIRE

The Institute for P-12 Engineering Research and Learning, or INSPIRE, the first major research concentration in the new school, was established through a generous five year funding commitment from the S. D. Bechtel, Jr. Foundation. INSPIRE was officially recognized as a Purdue University Center on March 3, 2006.

The founding vision was "*to create an engineering-literate society through preeminence in P-12 engineering education research and scholarship*" with a specific mission "*to construct theory on engineering thinking and learning and to inspire diverse students to pursue engineering and science for the benefit of humanity and the advancement of society*". In pursuit of this vision and mission, the work of the Institute was designed to integrate research and discovery, education and learning and engagement as three major pillars necessary to achieve its mission.

The 2005 Strategic Plan for INSPIRE set out the following guiding principles.

> *The key aspiration of INSPIRE is the creation of research-informed inclusive, integrative, equitable, and democratic learning opportunities and environments. INSPIRE seeks high quality research to develop theory and guide practice. Diversity, teamwork, professionalism, accountability, ethics, honesty, compassion, pride, respect, and courtesy are attributes that are most important as people of INSPIRE carry out their roles, empowering themselves and INSPIRE to fulfill its vision and mission.*

INSPIRE had the following seven goals, each with a corresponding set of operational strategies.

> *Goal 1 Theoretical Understanding: Conduct basic multidisciplinary research in human cognition and concept development in engineering education to inform curriculum development, learning environments, and teacher education.*

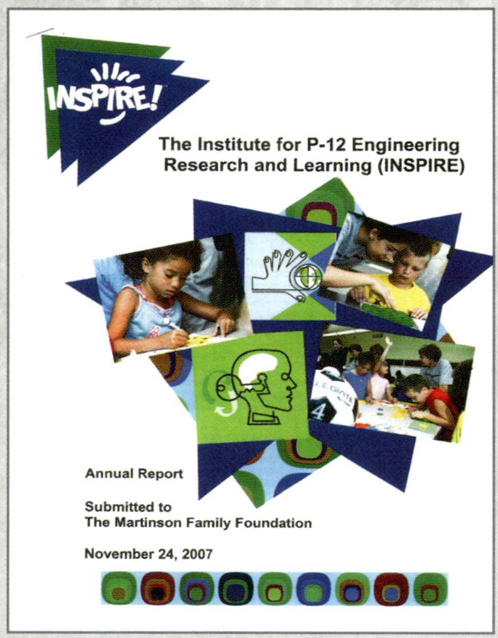

2015 ↓ INSPIRE Team Members

↓ The first P-12 Engineering and Design Education Research Summit in Seaside, Oregon, August 2010

↓ Teachers Amy Freeman and Mandy Center working through a project at the 2015 INSPIRE Teacher Academy

↓ INSPIRE new logo and branding launched in June 2015

↓ Two preschoolers, daughters of Elizabeth Gajdzik and Darshini Render, respectively, build a house using Tinkertoy parts featured in the 2015 Engineering Toy Guide

Goal 2 Bridging Theory to Practice: Apply results from basic research to the design of engineering curriculum, student learning environments, and teacher education.

Goal 3 Teacher Education: Provide teachers with research-informed opportunities to broaden their perspectives of the nature and practice of engineering; change the way they think about their students, their teaching, and learning environments and experiences; and gain confidence and skills in teaching with developmentally appropriate engineering curriculum (e.g. open-ended problems).

Goal 4 Engineering Curriculum: Develop and promote adaptable theory-based curricular opportunities and their ties to engineering education through developmentally-appropriate curriculum that keys on mathematics, science and technology.

Goal 5 Outreach: Build and maintain strong partnerships with educational constituents to grow a vital and consistent platform for research and translation of research results to formal classroom implementation.

Goal 6 Assessment & Evaluation: Develop, adapt, and apply assessment and evaluation systems that measure the impact of theory-based INSPIRE teacher education, engineering curricula, and student learning initiatives upon formal and informal educational constituents.

Goal 7 Policy: Initiate and lead an advocacy effort with state and national levels to inform and influence policy-making that will increase the U.S. commitment to P-12 engineering education.

"The Kurz Atrium is made possible by a gift from Herman and Heddy Hurz. Herman (BSEE '25) always valued his Purdue education and the solid foundation it provided him throughout his life. Herman's legacy continues as Heddy lends her helping hands to Purdue Engineering by supporting the world-class facilities necessary to educate the engineers of tomorrow." Dedication plaque

↓ Herman and Heddy Kurz Atrium

↓ First-Year Engineering Advising Lobby

↓ Amelia's Cafe'

[2007]

ABOUT THIS SPREAD *Final stages and grand opening ceremony of the Neil Armstrong Hall of Engineering. Read more about Armstrong Hall on page 46.*

↓ Neil Armstrong and Gene Cernan, first and most recent people to walk on the moon, celebrate the opening of Armstrong Hall of Engineering

↓ Purdue astronauts at the opening of Armstrong Hall of Engineering on October 27, 2007

Department of Engineering Education moved to the Neil Armstrong Hall of Engineering

[2007]

Display features the three programs to promote Engineering Education at conferences and events

[2007] ENE *Strategic Plan* developed

New home for EPICS in Armstrong Hall of Engineering. Multidisciplinary Engineering students can do an EPICS project as their capstone design and many ENE faculty mentor EPICS teams.

Monica Cardella, Alice Pawley, David Radcliffe, Johannes Strobel
New Faculty Members

[2007]

CHAPTER 3
TRANSFORMATION 2008–2011

As a transformative community of scholars, we gather periodically to engage in reflective conversations about achievements, challenges and opportunities and to consider preferred futures. In the spirit of moving the field of engineering education forward, early on we adopted the name "Advance," rather than "Retreat," for such gatherings.

The original Research Advance was held in April 2005 with the then faculty plus some colleagues from Purdue and beyond. The growing faculty augmented with national and international colleagues participated in the Legacy Advance in December 2006. Possible legacy areas considered were; doctoral education, engineering education research; first-year engineering, strengthening partnerships with other units in Purdue, national and/or global leadership, being stewards and champions of the discipline of engineering education, multi-disciplinary capacity building and working at the interfaces.

This day-long event was followed by a series of mini-Advances in the spring of 2007 to continue and expand the dialogue on the graduate program, engineering education research, and first year engineering. In September 2007 the process for establishing a comprehensive strategic plan for the next decade and beyond began, leading to the ENE Strategic Advance held in January 2008. This event engaged a variety of stakeholders from ENE and Purdue including faculty, staff and students.

The eventual outcome was the ENE Strategic Plan 2008-2014 which adopted the mission for the School of Engineering Education as *transforming engineering education based on scholarship and research.*

Another outcome of these Advances was a process that ultimately led to the radical redesign of the engineering courses in the first-year engineering program, from two courses in the fall to one each in the fall and in the spring. The development of these new courses, to be taught in the imaginative Ideas to Innovation Learning Laboratory, was a multi-year, iterative process that involved every faculty member in the school plus many staff. The design of this radical new learning environment was conceived as the construction of Armstrong Hall was nearing completion. The week after the new building was officially opened by Neil Armstrong and Gene Cernan, large sections of the basement were demolished and the Ideas to Innovation Learning Laboratory was retrofitted. It opened for classes in fall 2008.

These courses and the new learning environment in Armstrong Hall were truly transformational. As with the curricula changes proposed by Dean Hawkins half a century earlier, these innovations were challenged and resisted by some, but with patience and sincerity, the faculty of the school pressed their points. To date over 16,000 students have each had two, semester-long, team-based, experiential learning classes as a foundation for developing professional habits of mind.

The Interdisciplinary Engineering Studies program was transformed through the accreditation of a BS degree in Multidisciplinary Engineering by ABET. The original design of this new degree included a number of systems-oriented courses focused on modeling in different domains and at multiple scales, an emphasis on professional development, management and entrepreneurship plus a capstone design experience.

First-year engineering students presenting their design concepts in the i2i laboratory

↓ First-year engineering students register at STAR (Summer Transition Advising and Registration) previously known as *Day on Campus*

↓ Engineering graduate students relax in Armstrong Hall

[2008]

February—Department of Engineering Education becomes the *School of Engineering Education*

↓ Members of the Academic Advisory Council for Engineering Education | LEFT TO RIGHT Wendy Newstetter, Barbara Olds, Keith Sawyer, Linda Katehi, Daryl E. Chubin, Jim Pellegrino (Chair) Dick Benson (See full council membership on page 117)

Multidisciplinary Engineering Program given ABET accreditation

Brent Jesiek
New Faculty Member

[2008]

↓ Removing glass wall to install AFL machinery into Armstrong Hall

↓ Bringing AFL equipment into Armstrong Hall through front wall

[2008]

ABOUT THIS SPREAD *The Artisan and Fabrication Laboratory (AFL) and the Ideas to Innovation Learning Laboratory (I2I) were retrofitted into the basement of Armstrong Hall in year after the building was opened.*

↓ Lowering AFL equipment down the stairwell near Amelia's Café

↓ Opening of the Ideas to Innovation Learning Laboratory

August—Ideas-to-Innovation (i2i) Learning Laboratory opens

Robin Adams and Monica Cox
NSF CAREER

David Bowker
CoE Leadership Award

[2008]

↓ First-year engineering students use unique design of B061 in Armstrong Hall to work as teams

[2008]

⇆ First-year engineering students working on design project in i2i laboratory

Johannes Strobel named Director of INSPIRE

[2008]

STRATEGIC PLAN

The Strategic Plan of the School of Engineering Education was developed in 2007-2008 using the methodology of Appreciative Inquiry, a highly iterative and inclusive process that engaged a broad range of stakeholders.

It **envisioned** *a more inclusive, socially connected and scholarly engineering education*. This implies that we radically rethink the boundaries of engineering and the purpose of engineering education. In pursuit of this vision, the **mission** of the School of Engineering Education is to *transform engineering education based on scholarship and research.*

The guiding tenets are:

- *Students first (in all we do)*
- *Integrity, respect, and trust in our dealings*
- *Balancing work with other commitments*
- *Being socially conscious in what we do and how we do it*
- *Strategic thinking, excellence, and accountability*

To achieve our mission we have **four goals:**

Empower our people: Empower all members of the School (students; professional, administrative, and clerical staff; academic advisors; and faculty) to contribute to the success of our integrated, multifaceted mission and to be leaders, advocates, and change agents over their lifetime. Empowerment rests upon a shared understanding of the vision, mission, goals, priorities, and capabilities of the School within the national and global landscape of engineering education. We are a continuous platform for members of engineering education community to engage, inform, and influence each other.

Set the pace (in innovative programs): Offer a full suite of undergraduate and graduate programs that set the global standard in engineering education grounded in and contributing to cutting-edge scholarship and research. The transformation of engineering begins when we challenge the fundamental assumptions behind engineering

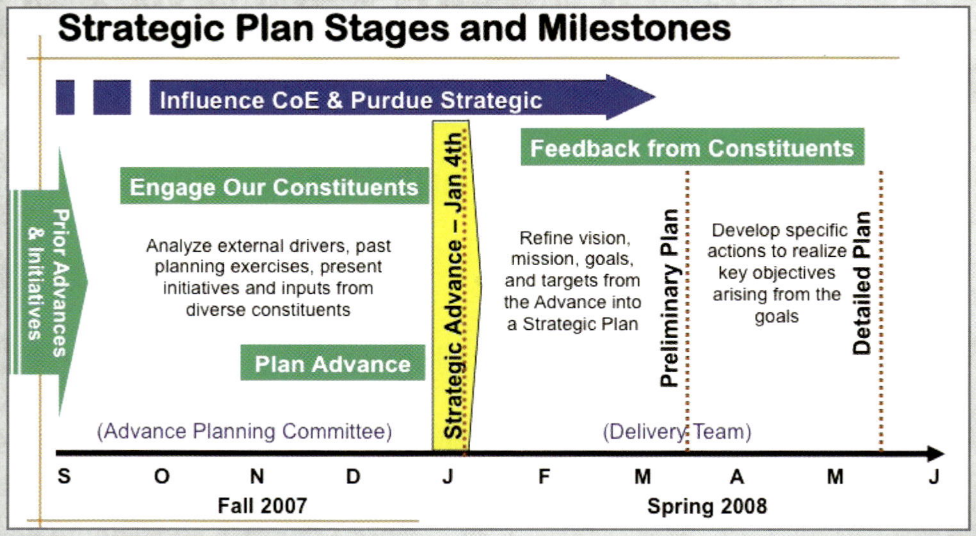

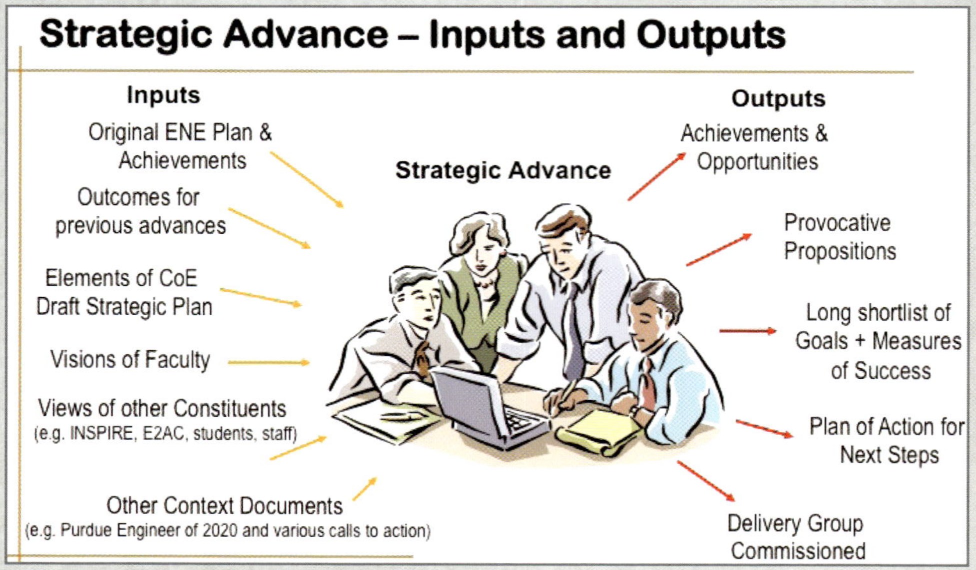

education and strive to create engineering programs that:

- *a.* *Diversify engineering: Open up engineering to a more diverse range of people by making their first experience of engineering (from Pre-College to 16) the most rewarding it can be;*
- *b.* *Embed creativity, innovation, and social responsibility: Create an understanding of the essential nature of engineering as creative and as contributing to a better world; and*
- *c.* *Enrich the student experience: Determine what information, advice, preparation, pedagogies, and learning experiences attract, retain, and grow global engineers.*

Tackle the big research questions: Create a world-renowned interdisciplinary research concentration at Purdue that addresses the big questions and challenges facing STEM education, with particular emphasis on engineering. Use our unique infrastructure and capability to be a pathfinder based on systematic research, policy development, and assessment. Reshape the research agenda by asking questions that challenge fundamental assumptions about engineering education across both the span of life and the different modes of participation in engineering. Influence the direction of and resource allocation for engineering education scholarship nationally and internationally.

Grow the (broader engineering education research and innovation) community: Identify and build strategic global partnerships and collaborations to elevate our research capabilities and those of the wider engineering education community, while simultaneously facilitating the sharing of experiences across the global community of engineering education scholars. Each of the four goals is accomplished progressively via a rolling set of initiatives. At the ENE Advance each May, we review current initiatives and initiate new ones as needed and set specific priorities and targets over three horizons; one year, three years and five years.

The essential elements of this plan—the vision, mission, values and goals—have stood the test of time.

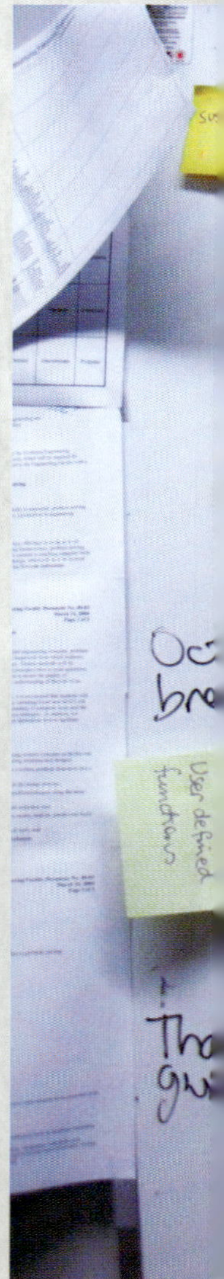

↓ Engineering Education Research Advance

[2009]

Krishna Madhavan and Senay Purzer
New Faculty Members

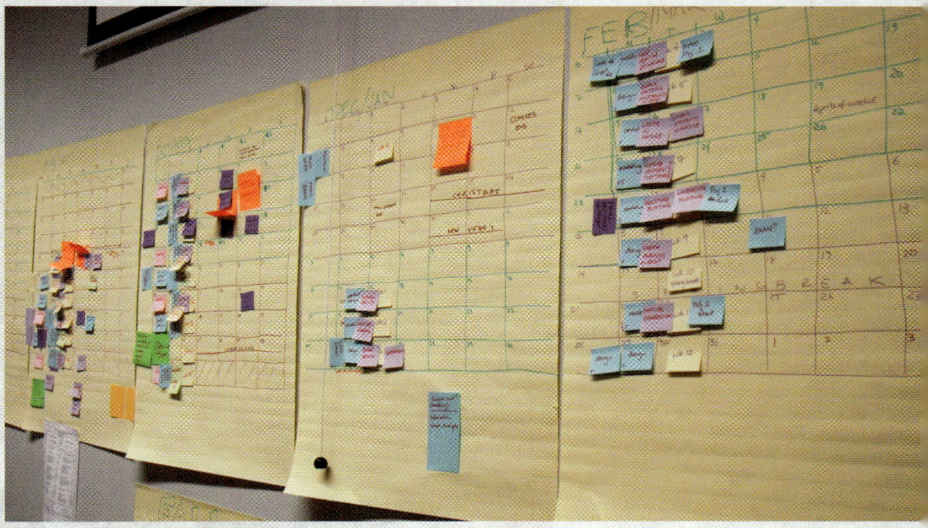

Grassroots planning exercise for the development of the new team-based First-Year Engineering courses ENGR 131/132 and ENGR 141/142

June—David Radcliffe named Interim Head of the School of Engineering Education

[2009]

↓ First-year honors students test their roof top robots in the Demonstration Studio of the Ideas to Innovation Learning Laboratory

[2009]

August—New First-Year Courses implemented for 2009-2010 academic school year

National symposium held in Washington DC in September to stimulate a dialogue amongst engineering Deans on establishing engineering education opportunities in colleges of engineering. Co-led by Purdue, Virginia Tech, Utah State and Clemson the symposium highlighted opportunities and challenges based on the early experience of these four institutions with engineering education programs.

↓ Faculty participating in the national symposium

↓↑ Engineering Education Outstanding Alumni | TOP Teri Reed-Rhodes addresses guests at awards ceremony; BOTTOM RECIPIENTS Robert Sharpe, Jr., Gary Horlacher, Brian Farley, Mary Smith, Harold Aberman

Robert Sharpe, Jr., Gary Horlacher, Brian Farley, Mary Smith, and Harold Aberman
Outstanding Alumni Award

Eric Holloway
College of Engineering New Employee Award

[2009]

⭣ Dean Jamieson leads celebrations to mark the fifth anniversary of the School of Engineering Education, April 9, 2009

[2009]

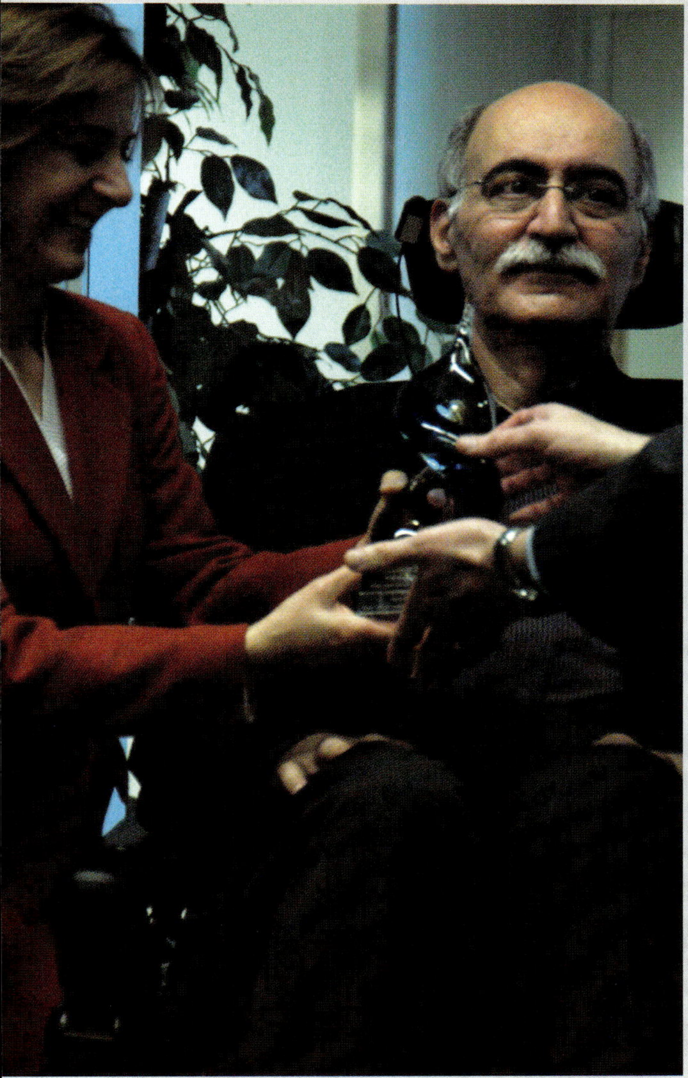

⇣ Atossa Rahmanifar and Kamyar Haghighi accept award in recognition as founding head

⇣ Engineering Education Singers perform at the fifth anniversary | LEFT TO RIGHT Amy Glenn, David Bowker, Nathan McNeill, Alice Pawley, Matt Ohland, Shawn Jordan and Lisa Tally

[2009]

CHAPTER 3 FEATURE

IDEAS TO INNOVATION LEARNING LABORATORY

A transformational change in instruction in first-year engineering occurred in 2008 with the creation of the Ideas to Innovation Learning Laboratory or i2i in Armstrong Hall. Instead of being one of 400 or more in an impersonal lecture theater, students became a member of a four person team. This imaginative learning environment enabled the adoption, on a vast scale not attempted previously, of experiential learning centered on teamwork and active and collaborative learning techniques, a pedagogy based on research evidence. The i2i learning laboratory was a precursor of the IMPACT classrooms now deployed across Purdue.

The following extracts from a prospectus, prepared in December 2007, capture the concept of the Ideas to Innovation Learning Laboratory. This proposal led to support from the S. D. Bechtel, Jr. Foundation to help realize this vision.

The Department of Engineering Education at Purdue University proposes the creation of the Ideas to Innovation (I2I) Learning Laboratory Complex, a unique, flexible space that will engage learners of all ages in creating solutions to stimulating, authentic design challenges that require creative and innovative thinking.

The goal is to make engineering come alive for Purdue's engineer, as well as for students involved in our pre-college outreach initiatives, by placing the entire design and innovation process at the center of learning. Through the combined use of space, state-of-the-art learning technologies, and advanced fabrication equipment, we will significantly augment the learner's firsthand experience with engineering concepts and contexts and provide the foundation for future exploration and motivation of sophisticated engineering thinking.

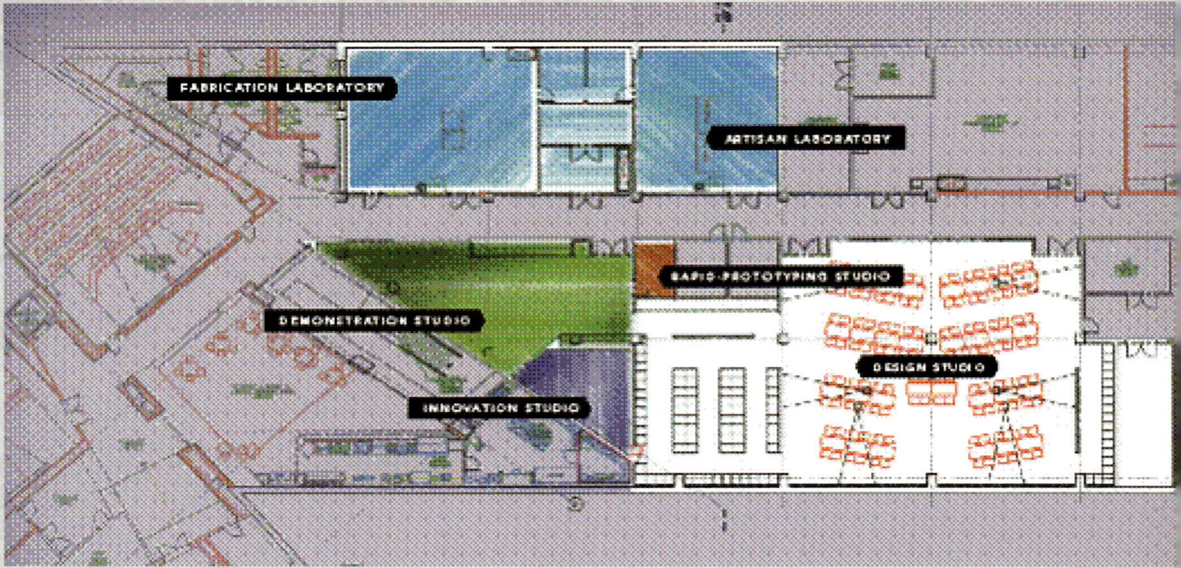

↓ Activity specific spaces that comprise the Ideas to Innovation Learning Laboratory

↓ Ideas to Innovation Learning Laboratory Design Cycle

↓ Fabrication Laboratory where students help fellow students to realize their design ideas

↓ Artwork communicates the Ideas to Innovation Learning Laboratory concept

↓ Bold signage identify specific spaces

The fundamental premise of the I2I Learning Laboratory is that optimal learning for young engineers occurs when the learning environment centers on the students, provides collaboration with peers, and allows for hands-on experience with engineering tools and processes to explore authentic problems. In the I2I Learning Laboratory, students will experience the entire engineering design process. The team-focused, collaborative spaces—the Design Studio, Innovation Studio, Rapid-Prototyping Studio, Fabrication and Artisan Laboratories, and Demonstration Studio—form a physical representation of the design cycle, serving as a constant reminder to students to ask questions and define the goals of success (design criteria), invent potential alternatives, anticipate and plan for a chosen option, build a prototype and test, reflect based on evaluative outcomes, and refine as needed.

Our goal is to make engineering come alive for Purdue's engineer, as well as those involved in our pre-college outreach initiatives, by keying on the entire design and innovation process. Through the combined use of space, state-of-the-art learning technologies, and advanced fabrication equipment, we will significantly augment the learner's firsthand experience with engineering concepts and contexts and provide the foundation for future exploration and motivation of sophisticated engineering thinking.

... as technology and the engineering students of tomorrow continue to change, the space in which the students learn must be flexible and reflect the state-of-the-art environment engineers live in as professionals in today's fast-changing world. Ultimately, an enabling environment for engineering students to experience engineering design, creativity, and innovation in a gateway course that is part of their required curriculum.

Wall art features the original logo and branding

↓ INSPIRE wall art in Grissom Hall, the second office location for the research institute from 2010-2014

↓ Graduate Open House to introduce prospective students to the faculty, graduate students and research in Engineering Education, October | Michele Strutz and Joe Lin

[2010]

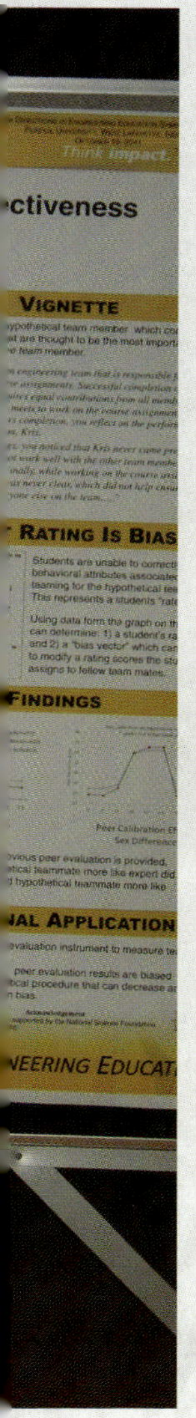

Tosin Ogunwuyi, DeLean Tolbert, Alice Pawley and Kelsey Rogers at Graduate Open House

Graduate Open House Poster Session in Armstrong Hall Kurz Atrium

David Radcliffe named the Kamyar Haghighi Head of Engineering Education

[2010]

↓ Engineering Education Outstanding Alumni Recipient Howard Gobstein with David Radcliffe, Phillip Wankat and Dean Leah Jamieson

[2010]

Howard Gobstein
Outstanding Alumni Award

↓ Monica Cox (second row, third from center) at the White House ceremony for Presidential Early Career Awards for Scientists and Engineers

↓ Geoff Crowley (IDE 1974) recognized as a Distinguished Engineering Alumnus

Monica Cox
NSF PECASE Recipient

Alice Pawley
NSF CAREER

[2010]

↓ Dean Leah Jamieson with Kamyar Haghighi

↓ Former Purdue President Martin Jischke congratulates Kamyar Haghighi

[2010]

ABOUT THIS SPREAD *Announcing the Named Headship for the School of Engineering Education in honor of the founding head Kamyar Haghighi and funded by the S.D. Bechtel, Jr. Foundation.*

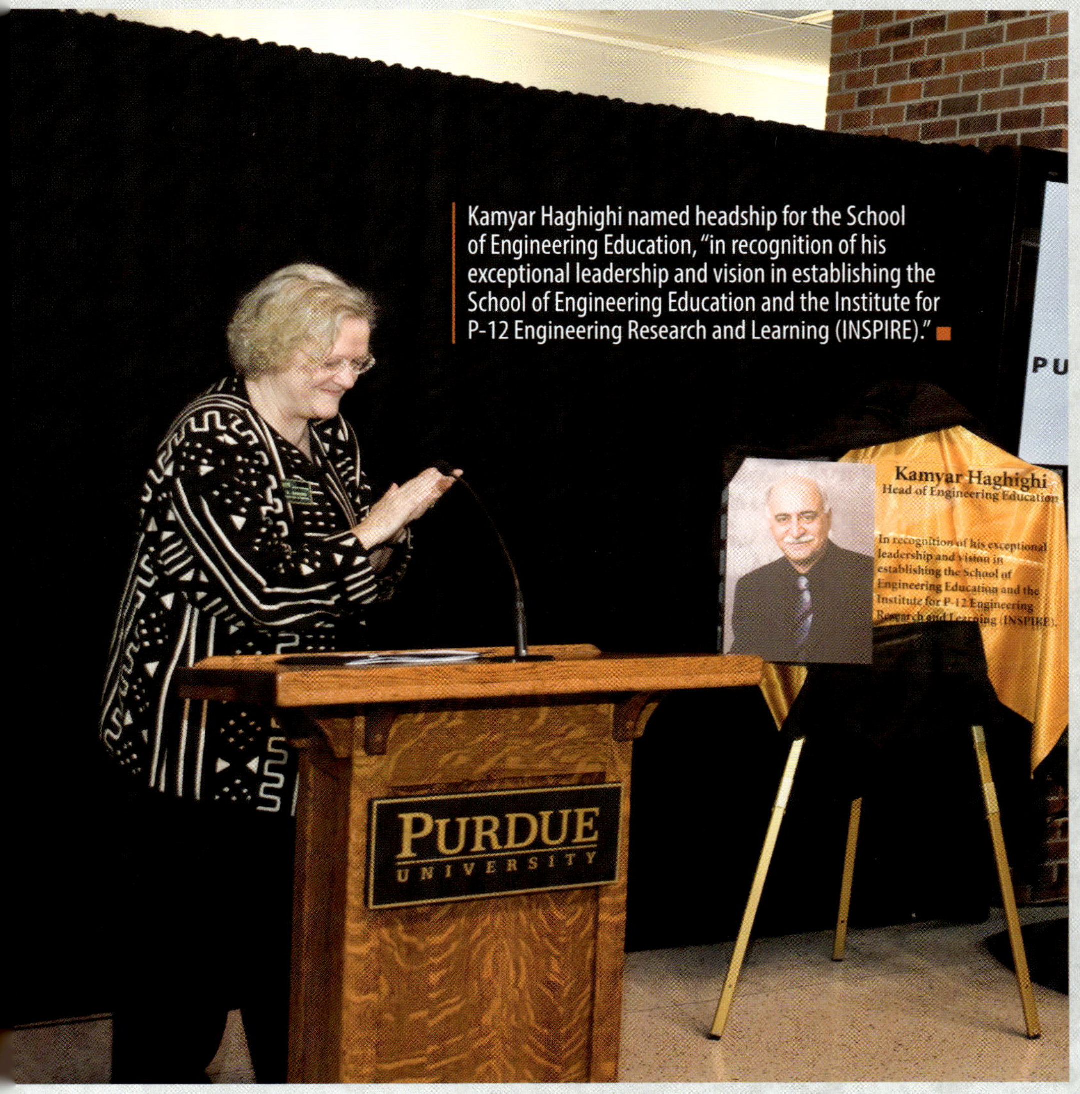

Kamyar Haghighi named headship for the School of Engineering Education, "in recognition of his exceptional leadership and vision in establishing the School of Engineering Education and the Institute for P-12 Engineering Research and Learning (INSPIRE)." ■

↓ Dean Leah Jamieson presents new headship in honor of Kamyar Haghighi

↓↑ TOP AND BOTTOM | Many engineering faculty, staff, and guests attend the headship announcement event

[2010]

MULTIDISCIPLINARY ENGINEERING

Forming the Department of Engineering Education by the merging of Freshman Engineering and the Division of Interdisciplinary Engineering Studies (IDES) program was a master stroke. Having its own BS program as well as the graduate program made it a complete school like others in the college. However the IDES degree program needed to be reimagined.

> *By the early 21st century it was evident that IDES was serving two groups of students. One group of students wanted an engineering education but did not plan to pursue an engineering career. For example, these students were in pre-professional programs such as premedical engineering or prelaw engineering. The non-ABET accredited program was a good fit for these students. The other group of students was interested in pursuing an engineering career in programs such as acoustical engineering, biomedical engineering, and engineering management.*
>
> *Graduates who followed careers that did not require them to become registered professional engineers had few complaints about their educational preparation. On the other hand, graduates who wanted to become professional engineers often had considerable difficulty in being allowed to take the professional engineering examination because they had not graduated from an ABET accredited program. (Until 2006 IDES had a waiver from the Indiana State Board that allowed seniors in IDES to take the Fundamentals of Engineering exam.) It was clear that students who planned to practice engineering would be better served if an ABET accredited program were available.*
>
> *Remaking a non-accredited program into an accredited program is a nontrivial undertaking...Since the non-accredited IDES program served the needs of one group of students, we decided to retain this program while developing a new Multidisciplinary Engineering program that met ABET's accreditation standards. Fortunately, the*

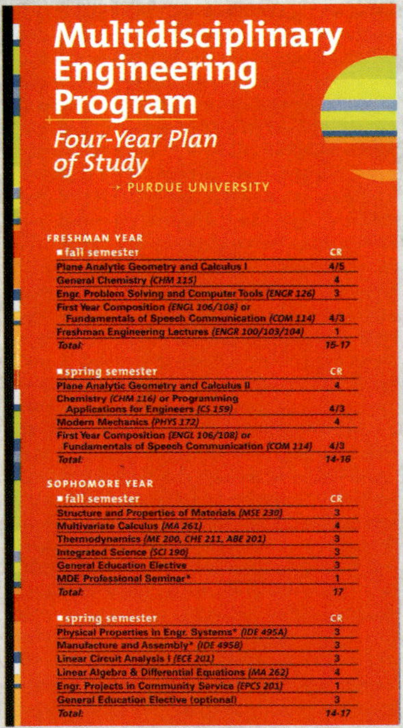

Multidisciplinary Engineering Program

Four-Year Plan of Study

→ PURDUE UNIVERSITY

FRESHMAN YEAR

■ fall semester	CR
Plane Analytic Geometry and Calculus I	4/5
General Chemistry *(CHM 115)*	4
Engr. Problem Solving and Computer Tools *(ENGR 126)*	3
First Year Composition *(ENGL 106/108)* or Fundamentals of Speech Communication *(COM 114)*	4/3
Freshman Engineering Lectures *(ENGR 100/103/104)*	1
Total:	*15-17*

■ spring semester	CR
Plane Analytic Geometry and Calculus II	4
Chemistry *(CHM 116)* or Programming Applications for Engineers *(CS 159)*	4/3
Modern Mechanics *(PHYS 172)*	4
First Year Composition *(ENGL 106/108)* or Fundamentals of Speech Communication *(COM 114)*	4/3
Total:	*14-16*

SOPHOMORE YEAR

■ fall semester	CR
Structure and Properties of Materials *(MSE 230)*	3
Multivariate Calculus *(MA 261)*	4
Thermodynamics *(ME 200, CHE 211, ABE 201)*	3
Integrated Science *(SCI 190)*	3
General Education Elective	3
MDE Professional Seminar*	1
Total:	*17*

■ spring semester	CR
Physical Properties in Engr. Systems* *(IDE 495A)*	3
Manufacture and Assembly* *(IDE 495B)*	3
Linear Circuit Analysis I *(ECE 201)*	3
Linear Algebra & Differential Equations *(MA 262)*	4
Engr. Projects in Community Service *(EPCS 201)*	1
General Education Elective (optional)	3
Total:	*14-17*

↓ Plan of Study brochure insert

↓ Wordle showing how MDE students perceive their unique strengths

↓ Multidisciplinary Engineering capstone design class

↓ Christine Pekny, Interdisciplinary Engineering Program Advisor, with student honoree Stephen Kelly and his parents at the 2012 Outstanding Alumni Awards dinner celebration

↓ Phil Wankat with 2010 student award winners Carmen Rodriguez, Philip Zumbrun and Nichole Schrank

↓ IDE alum Howard Gobstein (second from right) with Mary Pilotte meet with current generation of students Alex Offenbach, Abby Lemert and Sara Harman

↓ Current and former directors of the IDE program | LEFT TO RIGHT Phil Wankat, Mary Pilotte and Dick Grace

university already had approval from the state to offer both a Bachelor of Science in Engineering (BSE) degree and a Bachelor of Science (BS) degree – otherwise, significant time and effort would be required to achieve this approval. The BSE degree was reserved for MDE students. Both programs are restricted to areas that are not covered by traditional engineering programs at the university.

In developing the MDE curriculum the decision was made to retain the basic idea that students would take the majority of their engineering courses outside of the MDE program. This decision greatly increases program flexibility and decreases the costs of a new program, but it adds the difficulty of how to ensure that students are satisfying the program outcomes. A multi-faceted assessment program was developed based on extensive assessments in two courses, encouraging students to take the Fundamentals of Engineering exam, an oral examination conducted by the Industrial Advisory Council, and an extensive exit interview.

Without controlling courses, how does the MDE program ensure that all students meet the MDE program outcomes, that graduates meet the MDE program objectives, and how do we convince ABET that we have accomplished this? We have developed an assessment program that ensures all students satisfy the 12 outcomes of the MDE program. The outcomes were selected to ensure that graduates would meet the objectives of the MDE program (Table 4) and meet ABET criteria.
With the exception of the Industrial Advisory Council oral exam and the FE exam, we do not use sampling for assessments. Every student is assessed and the assessment for each student is recorded individually and each student is tracked individually to show that he or she satisfies all of the outcomes.

Wankat, P. and Haghighi, K. (2009) Multidisciplinary Engineering: Flexibility and ABET Accreditation, *Proceedings Annual Conference of ASEE*, Austin, Session 176.

↓ Engineering Education Outstanding Alumni Recipients Raymond Klein, Debra Echt and Richard Le Sesne

↓ INSPIRE receives CoE Team Award | LEFT TO RIGHT Senay Purzer, Dan Sommerville, Leah Jamieson, Vince Duffy, Melissa Dyehouse, Monica Cardella, Johannes Strobel, Nicole Weber, Sean Brophy, Elizabeth Gajdzik

[2011]

Raymond Klein, Debra Echt and Richard Le Sesne
Outstanding Alumni Award

INSPIRE
College of Engineering Team Award

In Remembrance of

Kamyar Haghighi

October 13, 1950 - May 9, 2011

Sunday, June 12, 2011
Thomas Duncan Hall
2:00 pm

Mozart String Quartet, K465 "Dissonance"

Welcome and Eulogy	**Farshid Eftekhari**
Gymnopedie No. 1, Satie	
Remarks	**Dr. David Radcliffe**
Gymnopedia No. 2, Satie	
Remarks	**Janice Eddy**
Gymnopedie No. 3, Satie	
Remarks	**Zia Fattahi**
Gnossienne No. 1, Satie	
Reflections	**Taraneh Rahmanifar**
Prelude from suite No. 1, Bach	
Reflections	**Audience**
Final Remarks	**Farshid Eftekhari**
Imagine, John Lennon	

Please join us for hors d'oeuvres and refreshments

Musicians

Deborah Rodin: Violin, Regan Eckstein: Violin, Amy Brandfonbrenner: Viola, Sara Wollan: Cello and Shellie Johnson: Piano

Ah, fill the Cup - what boots it repeat
How Time is slipping underneath our Feet:
Unborn Tomorrow, and dead Yesterday,
Why fret about them if Today be sweet!

از دی که گذشت هیچ از او یاد مکن
فردا که نیامده است فریاد مکن
برنامده و گذشته بنیاد مکن
حالی خوش باش و عمر بر باد مکن

- Omar Khayyam

"Kamyar Haghighi, the founding head of the School of Engineering Education, a professor of agricultural and biological engineering, and a national force for engineering education reform based on research and scholarship, died Monday, May 9, 2011, at the age of 60." Dr. Haghighi Obituary

INSPIRE launches *J-PEER*, an electronic journal for pre-college engineering education research

[2011]

NSF funded PEER Collaborative Workshop held in Athens GA (Co-PIs Alice Pawley, Senay Purzer and Nadia Kellam). Junior colleagues gather regularly to give each other advice, direction, and solace about their work as tenure-track faculty in engineering education. PEER stands for Pine Mountain Engineering Education Research, a reference to the state park in Kentucky where the genesis of this idea arose. ■

[2011]

Bill LeBold attends his 50th ASEE Meeting in Vancouver
Retired Faculty

"A special highlight of the meeting was the recognition of Bill LeBold who marked this meeting as the 50th meeting of ASEE that he has attended. That is a remarkable record and one that will not be easily broken." ASEE Academy of Fellows Newsletter, January 2012

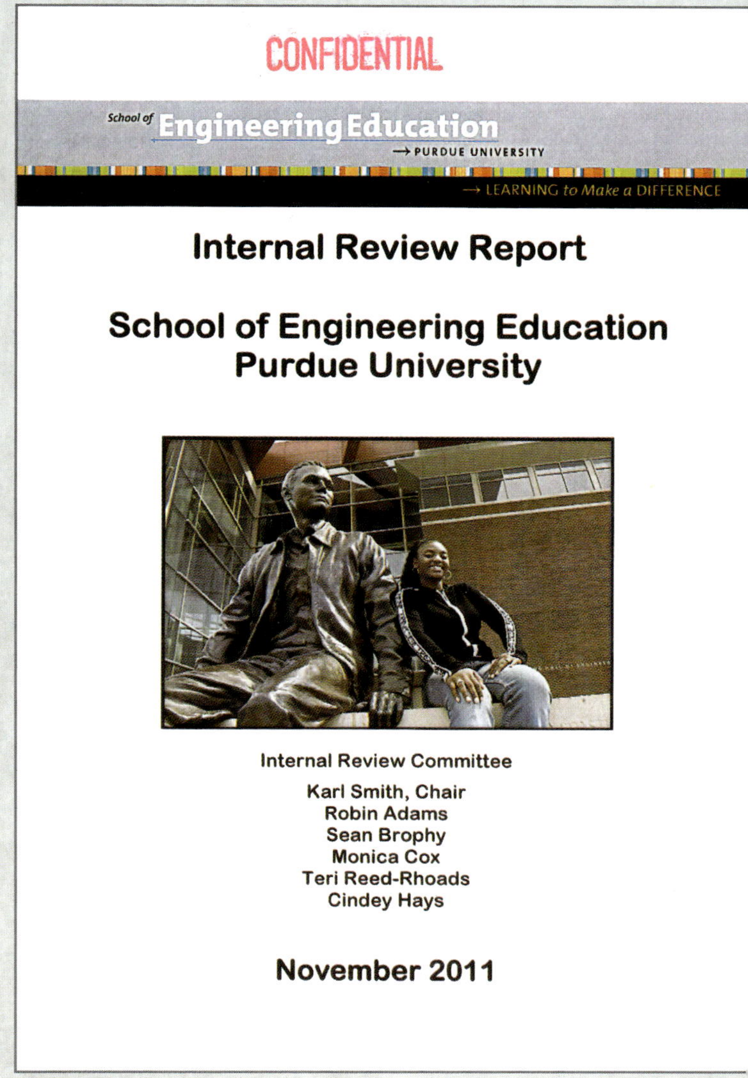

CONFIDENTIAL

School of Engineering Education
→ PURDUE UNIVERSITY
→ LEARNING to Make a DIFFERENCE

Internal Review Report

School of Engineering Education
Purdue University

Internal Review Committee

Karl Smith, Chair
Robin Adams
Sean Brophy
Monica Cox
Teri Reed-Rhoads
Cindey Hays

November 2011

↓ PhD students presenting at the annual Graduate Open House

↓ Report cover of self-study prepared for the successful first external review of the School of Engineering Education

Demetra Evangelou	Monica Cardella	Senay Purzer
NSF PECASE	NSF CAREER	NSF CAREER

[2011]

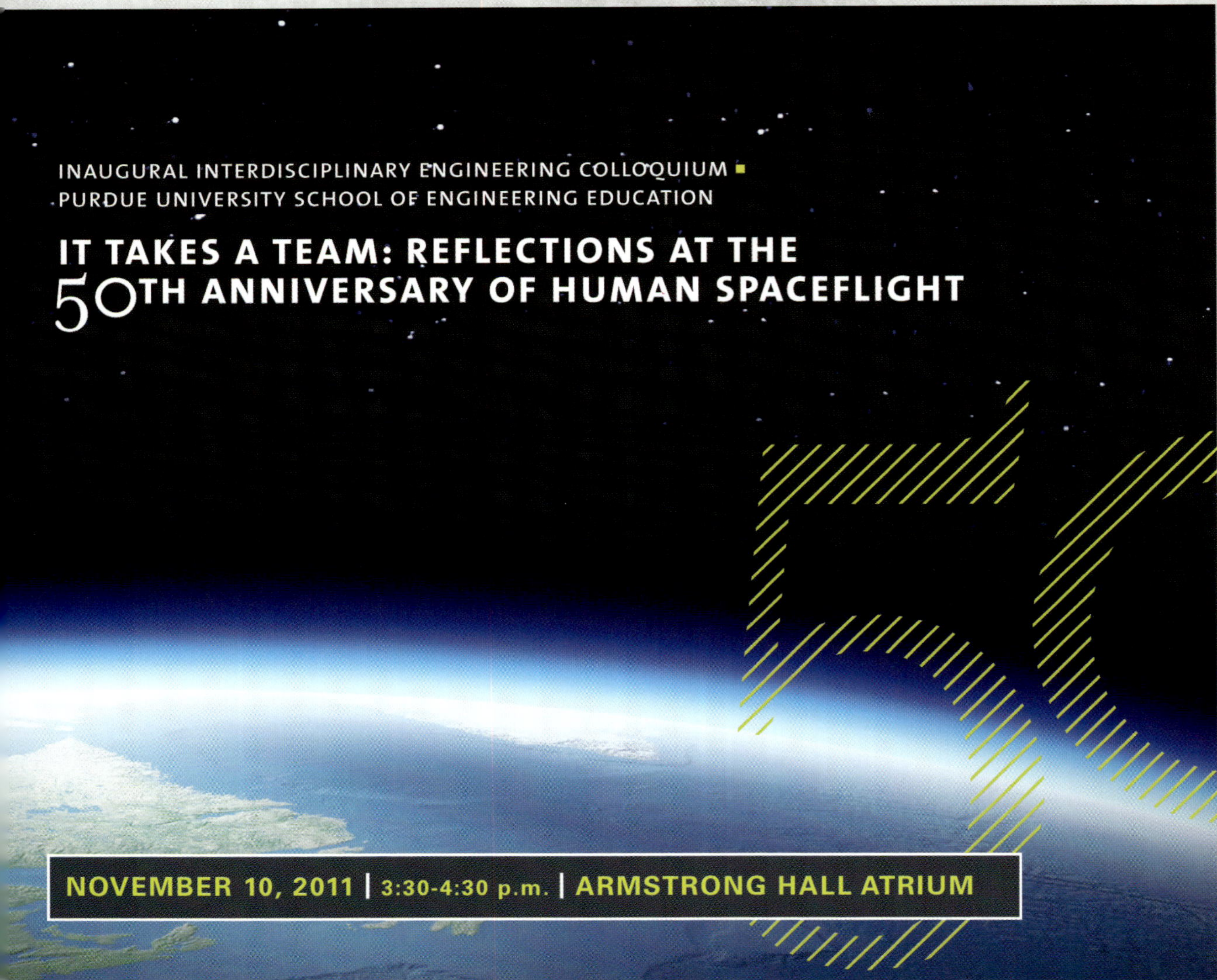

Inaugural colloquium invitation sent to Purdue engineering faculty, alumni and students for wide audience participation

[2011]

ABOUT THIS SPREAD *Inaugural Interdisciplinary Engineering Colloquium, an annual event created to present a topic of general interest from several disciplinary perspectives.*

↓ David Radcliffe provides opening remarks and introduces featured speakers Gary Horlacher (IDE alumni and NASA shuttle flight director) and Michael Smith, Purdue Professor of History

↓ Gary Horlacher and Michael Smith answers questions from colloquium participants

CHAPTER 4
IMPACT 2012–2016

During the era of Dean Hawkins, the early years of the Department of Freshman Engineering, engineering education underwent a fundamental paradigm shift in terms of *what* we teach, based on deeper engagement with the underpinning science as well as the art of engineering. These changes had a profound impact on every aspect of engineering education and the effects are still being felt today.

The School of Engineering Education is in the vanguard of the next fundamental transformation in engineering education this time centered on *how* we teach in relation to *how* students learn in the context of engineering. Grounded in educational and related research, this new wave of changes will have an impact comparable to that of the shift to the engineering sciences sixty years ago.

The 2012 ASEE report entitled *Innovation with Impact: Creating a Culture for Scholarly and Systematic Innovation in Engineering Education*, co-authored by Dean Leah Jamieson highlights this comparison.

> *Just as the engineering sciences transformed the curricula content in engineering education in the 1950s and 1960s, so the "Sputnik moment" for the current generation pivots on a transformation in the processes used to educate engineers to meet the challenges of our time.*

The founding head, Kamyar Haghighi, described the challenge in a 2005 guest editorial published in the *Journal of Engineering Education* in these terms.

> *The time of quiet crisis in engineering education is giving way to an intentional and visible paradigm shift in engineering attributes and outcomes, foundational research, and educational pedagogy..... Engineering education has been launched as a vital, vigorous, and scholarly academic discipline. ....We must conduct the research that leads to tools that define and transform the learning experience and must effectively incorporate technology into classrooms, including best practices for mentoring students in adapting to emerging technologies. We must underpin our program development and adaptation efforts with learning research in order to enhance diversity, encourage equity, and develop a long-term and successful recruiting pipeline. We can no longer afford, as British philosopher Bertrand Russell said, "an enterprise of methodical guessing" when it comes to educating our future engineers.*

Meeting this challenge required a clear vision, strategic allies, laser focus, determination, grit and resilience. Research-based innovations like the i2i learning laboratory have had a major impact on the first-year experience. In partnership with colleagues globally, our faculty have addressed many of the big research questions and created a field defining facility for engineering education research. However the most significant impact of this relatively new school is being felt through the leaders we grow; those people we nurture and develop and who go on to make a difference across their lifetime, at Purdue, across the United States and globally.

Tamara Moore utilizes a simulation classroom for her research in Engineering Education

↓ Rick Zadoks receives Engineering Alumni Loyalty Award

↓ The Neil Armstrong statue stages a gaze at the full moon featured on the annual alumni *thank you* card

[2012]

Rick Zadoks
Alumni Loyalty Award

Robin Adams
CoE Leadership Award

Lisa Tally
CoE Customer Service Award

Leslie Bottorff, Rick Kosdrosky
Outstanding Alumni Award

↓ Engineering Education Outstanding Alumni recipients Leslie Bottorff and Rick Kosdrosky with David Radcliffe

↓ Mike Gray (AAE 1958) filming video documentary in preparation for the tenth anniversary of the school

↓ Lisa Tally, Becky Fry, Mike Gray and David Radcliffe editing video documentary at Mike's home in Hollywood Hills, California

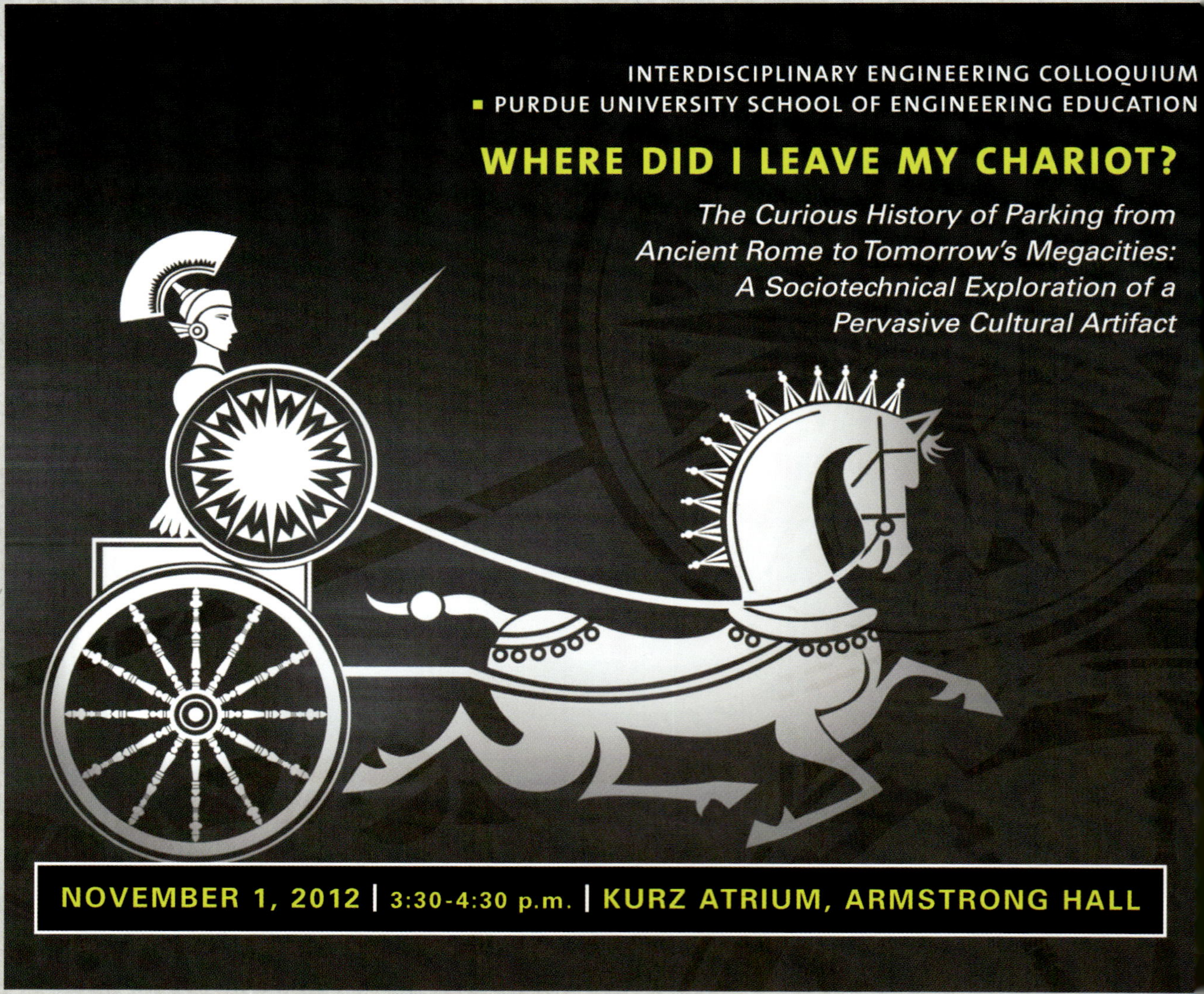

↓ Invitation for the Second Annual Interdisciplinary Colloquium

[2012]

⭳ Second Interdisciplinary Colloquium features IDE Alumnae Mary Smith (seated) and John Collier, Director of Campus Master Planning (podium)

⭳ Launching of the *Research Report* that features faculty research highlights

⭳ Accepting check from Delphi Corporation for advancing engineering education

↓ Inaugural class Harnessing Industry Expertise, co-taught by Rick Zadoks (right) and Monica Cox (third from left) the students are (left to right) Les Grundman, Tosin Ogunwuyi, Rui Pan, Mariana Tafur, Mary Pilotte

↓ Heidi Diefes-Dux and Kathleen Wible discuss best practices for classroom instruction with graduate students as part of the Teaching Undergraduates for Learning Investment Program or TULIP

[2012]

↓ The first P-12 Engineering and Design Education Research Summit organized by INSPIRE and held in Washington, D.C.

↓ Becky Fry, Director of Development, awaits the exhibition to open at the ASEE conference in San Antonio, Texas

Brent Jesiek	Alice Pawley	Senay Purzer
NSF CAREER	NSF PECASE	NSF CAREER

[2012]

FIRST-YEAR EXPERIENCE

An integral part of the School of Engineering Education, the First-Year Engineering (FYE) program is still the entry point for all beginning engineering students at Purdue. The mission of this student-oriented program is to advise, prepare, and retain students as they navigate the transition into college life and prepare to move to one of the sixteen engineering majors. Academic advisors are at the front line of guiding our first-year students, continuing a proud tradition that goes back to Freshman Engineering days.

> *Counselling continues to be important throughout the freshman year as students are permitted with academic advising to add courses, drop courses, or change the level of assignment even after classes begin. There is a three-part counselling staff to handle the wide variety of student needs each semester. The freshman engineering staff consists of the ten regular or full time counselors. These ten advisors maintain their offices in the Department of Freshman Engineering where they are assigned a 30 to 40 percent counselling duty. They also teach classes and have other responsibilities. Included as a regular part of the counselling staff are fifteen to twenty professors from the professional engineering schools who spend six to nine hours per week in the Freshman Engineering Department and are available to students who want detailed information about a specific program. The department also employs four to five junior or senior engineering students to serve as advisors to freshman students.*
>
> Butler, B.R. McDowell, R.W and LeBold, W.K (1978) Purdue Freshman Engineering Orientation, Placement, Counselling and Evaluation, *ERM*. Vol11 Issue: 1, pp 5-10, 29.

While the essential work of advising has not changed over the intervening decades, computers have transformed the day to day operations from how information is gathered, recorded and the way registration is done. Paper catalogs have

↓ 1980s First-Year Advising

↓ 2008 First-Year Advising

↓ 2009 Purdue Green Robotics competition located in the Kurz Atrium of Armstrong

↓ 2015 First-year engineering students attend their first engineering class, ENRG 131

↓ 2014 IDES Program Director Mary Pilotte talking with First-Year Engineers

↓ 2014-2015 First-Year Engineering Advising Team

↓ 2015 *Day on Campus* with FYE Advisors, Armstrong Hall

been replaced by online resources, web-based frequently asked questions supplement face-to-face encounters and students receive important information just-in-time via various social media and electronic bulletin boards.

Day on Campus has been superseded by STAR (Summer Transition, Advising and Registration). For students who cannot attend in person, there is Virtual STAR, an online experience designed for international students who live in vastly different time zones. In recent years over 20% of all entering first-year engineering students come from beyond our shores. To become more familiar with the transition issues involved our academic advisors have visited the home countries of these students.

Another significant change is that the Women in Engineering Program, the Minority Engineering Program and the First-Year Honors Program, all of which had their origins in Freshman Engineering, are now administered through the College.

Web-based learning management systems have transformed the classroom experience. Classes in the Ideas to Innovation Learning Laboratory have been "flipped", with the content being incorporated into online learning modules that can be viewed in the student's dorm room, or anywhere, at any time. The in-class time is focused on applying their new knowledge to projects and other class activities. Over the past six years electronic uploading of homework and assignments by students has replaced paper-based homework submissions in these courses; a significant change in the context of serving over 2000 students each semester.

⇣ Benjamin Ahn presents research poster at PhD in Engineering Education Graduate Open House

⇣ PhD in Engineering Education Graduate Open House Poster Session

[2013]

↓ Engineering Education Outstanding Alumni recipients Mary Smith, Howard Gobstein, Rick Kosdrosky and Richard Le Sesne visiting campus

↓ Engineering Education Outstanding Alumni recipients Stan Jones, Michael Wells and Eric Schmidt

William Oakes	**First-Year Engineering**	**Amanda Jackson**	**Stan Jones, Eric Schmidt, Michael Wells**
CoE A.A. Potter Award	CoE Staff Team Award	CoE Leadership Award	Outstanding Alumni Award

[2013]

↓ First-year engineering development team of staff and faculty is photographed for CoE Team Award | LEFT TO RIGHT Lynn Hegewald, Matt Ohland, Monica Cardella, Eric Holloway, Heidi Diefes-Dux, John Whitford , Patrick La Petina

↓ Engineering Education Research Advance | Using the talking wall, faculty brainstorm ideas for how best to grow the broader engineering education community

[2013]

Brent Jesiek
NSF CAREER

↓ Engineering Education Research Advance | Staff and faculty share their ideas about "being the best that we can be"

↓ Two pioneer faculty promoted to full professor, Heidi Diefes-Dux (left) and William Oakes (second from right) plus three junior faculty are tenured and promoted, Monica Cardella (second from left), Johannes Strobel (center) and Alice Pawley (right)

Morgan Hynes, Joyce Main, Tamara Moore, Mary Pilotte
New Faculty Members

[2013]

↓ ENE faculty and staff plan for Wang Hall features and research laboratory functionality

[2013]

↓ The 2013 colloquium kicked off the 10th anniversary celebration of the School of Engineering Education, featuring a panel discussion with LEFT TO RIGHT John Lindenlaub, Frank Oreovicz and Phillip Wankat

↓ Colloquiums are broadcast live through the Elliott Hall of Music services with videos archived on ENE's website

GLOBAL PARTNERSHIPS

Throughout the short history of this School, our faculty have played a vital role in catalyzing engineering education research, scholarship and innovation through partnerships with colleagues nationally and around the globe. This has taken the form of leadership in organizing various national and international conferences, colloquia and workshops.

Since 2004 our faculty have advanced a national community of practice grouped around developing knowledge and skills in rigorous research in engineering education and later workshops on cross-disciplinary collaborations. These and other capacity building activities have had a profound impact in growing and diversifying the engineering education community nationally.

The School of Engineering Education partnered with the other three existing departments of engineering education to conduct an NSF-funded national symposium in DC in March 2009 on opportunities for establishing similar academic programs in engineering education and was attended by twenty five deans of engineering, directors of engineering education centers, and educational researchers from various disciplines.

In 2012, the School initiated the first Engineering Education Research and Innovation cluster of booths in the exhibition hall of the annual American Society of Engineering Education Conference held in Vancouver. We have continued to coordinate this co-location of the academic units and research centers in engineering education at ASEE each summer, including the

2012 ↑ Invited speakers and host at the International Conference on Teaching and Learning in Higher Education at the Center for Engineering Education, University Teknologi Malaysia (UTM)

↑ Welcome banner in laboratories during a visit to Tsinghua University

2014 ↑ International colleagues meet at the School of Engineering Education booth at ASEE in Indianapolis

2011 ↑ Brent Jesiek on a visit to Beijing as part of a short-term study abroad initiative *Engineering Cultures East Asia*

2015 ↑ Jennifer DeBoer takes field notes in Kenya for research on engineering coursework that can help the children increase their employability

funding of a community zone. This gathering place is also a locus for international researchers in engineering education. We also coordinate a regular gathering of engineering education researchers and innovators at the annual ASEE and FIE conferences.

The school has also partnered with a variety of engineering education centers and groups around the world in research collaborations and capacity building. An early and enduring example is our relationship with the Universiti Teknologi Malaysia who in 2007 established a PhD in engineering education based on our program. We have also worked with Aalborg University, (Denmark); Aston University (Birmingham, UK); Beihang University (Beijing, China); Hong Kong University for Science and Technology, KTH Royal Institute of Technology (Stockholm, Sweden), Sungkyunkwan University, plus other universities who are members of the Korean Innovative Engineering Education network and Tsinghua University (Beijing, China). New partnerships are emerging in Latin America and Africa.

Our faculty have been invited by the major global engineering education associations to give keynote presentations; these include the Australasian Association for Engineering Education (AaeE), the European Society for Engineering Education (SEFI), the International Society for Engineering Pedagogy (IGIP), Korean Society of Engineering Education (KSEE) and the South African Society for Engineering Education (SASEE) and numerous other international conferences.

↓ Engineering Education Outstanding Alumni recipient Rex Carter with David Radcliffe and Phillip Wankat

↓ The West Lafayette High School quartet traditionally plays at each Outstanding Alumni Awards dinner

[2014]

Rex Carter
Outstanding Alumni Award

ENE Safety Committee
Presidential Safety Award

Monica Cox
CoE Leadership Award

↓ The School of Engineering Education celebrating ten years with an open house event held in the Kurz Atrium located in Armstrong Hall for the College of Engineering

↓ Phillip Wankat and John Gaunt attending the open house

[2014]

↓ ASEE in Indianapolis, Indiana features an engineering education research & innovation meeting area located in the convention center

[2014]

Monica Cardella named INSPIRE Director
Mary Pilotte named Director of Interdisciplinary Undergraduate Program

⭣ Visiting scholar, Jian Lin Vice, Director of Center for Engineering Education, Tsinghau University talks with students in first-year engineering class

⭣ First-year engineering advisors Nathan Thomas and Billi Jennings visit with families at Purdue Family Day

Ed Berger, Jennifer DeBoer, Allison Godwin, Michael Loui
New Faculty Members

[2014]

↓ Engineering Education wins the Presidential Safety Award for 2014 | Members of the safety committee were Patrick La Petina, Jeff Huddleston, Jim Whitford and Rick Womack together with Eric Holloway, the previous chair of the committee

⇣ Interdisciplinary Colloquium "Risky Business" feature speakers Tom Gray, Property Consulting Director, CNA and Karen Marais, Assistant Professor, Purdue School of Aeronautics and Astronautics

⇣ Design Theory Research Symposium | This symposium involves sharing a common research dataset of design review conversations: videos of conversations between those who give and those who receive feedback, guidance or critique during a design review

Tamara Moore
NSF PECASE

[2014]

↓ Junior faculty from engineering education programs around the US participate in the 2014 PEER Collaborative workshop at Purdue as part of our tenth anniversary celebrations

[2014]

↓ PhD graduate Velvet Fitzpatrick celebrates with her family on commencement day

↓ Commencement for ENE students, both undergraduate and graduate, are celebrated each year with faculty and staff in the School of Engineering Education offices

RESEARCH FACILITIES

A ground breaking facility dedicated to research in engineering education was opened in 2015.

When the School of Engineering Education at Purdue was formed in April 2004, no provision was made for research space. After moving into the newly completed Armstrong Hall of Engineering in fall 2007, the only space dedicated to research activities was 1500 sq. ft. to house graduate students and research staff. There was an implicit assumption that the research in engineering education took place in existing class rooms, so there was no need for dedicated laboratory space. While this was the case for some, other members of this growing faculty and their graduate students who gathered data through interview techniques simply booked every available room or spare office in Armstrong Hall and adjacent buildings for this purpose and to hold their research group meetings.

As each new faculty joined the School of Engineering Education from 2005 onwards they had the option to request space for research purposes from the College on a 3-5 year lease on a case-by-case basis. Some faculty requested space and were granted it; some did not request space. By 2012 the total of research space was 2700 sq.ft., scattered over 5 or 6 separate locations in multiple buildings across the whole engineering precinct. The Institute for Pre-College Engineering (INSPIRE) was initially allocated a small amount of office space in Hampton Hall. INSPIRE quickly out grew this space so in 2009 it moved to the top floor of Grissom Hall.

In 2013, as part of the growth of Purdue Engineering, an opportunity arose for the School of Engineering

↓ Wang Hall blanketed with the first snow of 2015

↓ The ENE community gather in Wang Hall for an opening ceremony

↓ Shortly after Wang Hall opens its doors, Dean Jamieson hosted the EAC dinner in the commons

⇣ Laboratory designed with one-way glass to observe teams at work | Nick Fila and Justin Hess

⇆ Examples of the flexible spaces designed to foster collaboration | LEFT Fabrication Lab with Cole Joslyn and Mel Chua; MIDDLE Collab Suite with Dan Ferguson, Susan Lord and Matt Ohland; RIGHT Simulation Classroom with Nicholas Morris

Education to acquire a 17,000 sq. ft. space in Wang Hall to house all current and future research activities. Having all our research be co-located for the first time also gave the faculty, students and research staff the opportunity to explore ways to better integrate the variety of work we do plus the opportunity to learn more about each other's work and to learn from each other more directly.

A user-centered design approach led to the emergence of an integrated cluster of research spaces in Wang Hall. Rather than create separate laboratories for each faculty member or thematic group, as happens in other engineering departments, we designed a series of multi-purpose spaces that could be flexibly re-purposed and re-assigned based on changing needs over time. There are spaces; (i) to meet to plan research, manage projects and to present findings, (ii) to collect data, (iii) to analyze data and manage projects, (iv) to store critical data and associated documents, (v) to gather as a community and also hold exhibitions and displays and (vi) for private meetings. Most internal walls are glass from floor to ceiling, allowing daylight to penetrate into the central part of the building, providing a visual sense of transparency and to foster collaboration.

There is a "simulation classroom" suite, three rooms with movable walls that can operate singly or together plus a fab-lab (maker space) all of which can be observed while in use. In addition to the smart suites, there is a large, open-layout space for graduate students with desks, a lounge area, an eating area adjacent to the full kitchen plus a quiet study room and a student meeting room.

Radcliffe, D.F. (2015) Creating a Large, Integrated and Flexible Engineering Education Research Facility, *Proceedings Research in Engineering Education Symposium*, Dublin.

↓ David Radcliffe with Outstanding Alumni recipient Henry Frissora

↓ Krishna Madhavan and his students working on an interactive, web-based knowledge visualization tool

[2015]

Henry Frissora
Outstanding Alumni Award

Cindey Hays
CoE Professional Achievement Award

Wang Hall research facility opens

↓ Joyce Main tests a First-Year engineering student group race track design that were demonstrated for play at the Patty Jischke Early Care and Education Center

↓ Ruth Streveler presents graduate students with achievement awards | LEFT TO RIGHT Nichole Ramirez, Ruth Streveler, Catherine Berdanier, Kelsey Rogers

↓ The 2015 PhD student cohort, known as Explorers in the first semester, with Steve Hoffmann after presenting their First-Year focused research projects at the weekly research seminar series | LEFT TO RIGHT Dhinesh Radhakrishnan, David Evenhouse, Hoda Ehsan, Anthony Lowe, Chanel Beebe, Richard Aleong, Nathan Hicks, Steve Hoffmann

Phillip Wankat
College of Engineering Celebration of Faculty Careers Colloquium

↓ Ed Berger visits with a first-year engineering student and his family at the Purdue University football game *Family Day* annual event

↓ The 2015 Interdisciplinary Colloquium features Purdue Professors of Engineering Practice with a live panel and pre-filmed video interviews | Shown here are Professors of Engineering Practice Bob Kenley (left), Dan Dumbacher (center) and Brad Duerstock (right) with host Mary Pilotte, IDE Program Director

[2015]

Jennifer DeBoer
NSF CAREER

Morgan Hynes
NSF CAREER

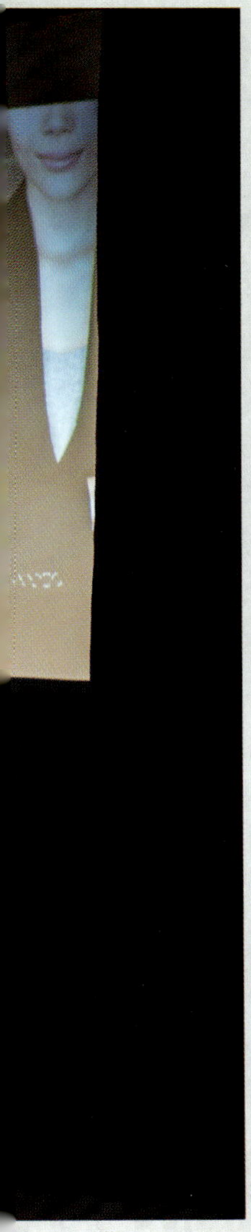

↓ Audeen Fentiman is named the Crowley Family Professor in Engineering Education by Debasish (Deba) Dutta, Purdue Provost

↓ Monica Cardella, Nadia Aljabi, Elizabeth Gajdzik and Terri Sanger release the second annual engineering gift guide at the Explorer Toys toy store in Zionsville, Indiana

Faculty attend the annual Frontiers in Education conference | LEFT Karl Smith and ENE alumni Rocio Chavela Guerra discussing engineering education practices with colleagues across different universities
RIGHT ENE Alumni Noah Salzman, graduate student Amy Van Epps, Marisa Orr (LTU) and Matt Ohland

Allison Godwin (center) talks with potential PhD students during the annual Graduate Open House

Brent Jesiek and Michael Loui helping at the ENE booth at Frontiers in Education Conference in El Paso, Texas

[2015]

⇣ Students Sonja Adams, Sara Harman, IDE Program Director Mary Pilotte, and student Alex Offenbach skating at the Riverside Skating Center as part of an IDE community event

⇣ Cindey Hays (left), longtime administrative assistant to the head of ENE is recipient of the Professional Achievement Award

⇣ IDE welcomes students in its first homeroom located in the Armstrong Hall 1300 suite. The new space brings together all current students who vary in IDE and MDE majors and classes. Students named the homeroom **The Nest**.

Audeen Fentiman, Muhsin Menekse
New Faculty Members

[2015]

↓ Korean visitors led by Soobong Shin (second from right), Professor from the Department of Civil Engineering at INHA University, with Brent Jesiek, Mary Pilotte and David Radcliffe

↓ INSPIRE Community Coordinator Terri Sanger (middle) and ENE graduate students present at the inaugural CAT-Purdue STEM Opportunity Fair at the Caterpillar plant in Lafayette

↓ David Radcliffe and graduate student Juan Ortega-Alvarez exchange sentiments and laughs at the conclusion of David's presentation for the College of Engineering Faculty Colloquium Series | front row graduate students LEFT TO RIGHT Richard Aleong, Nick Stites, Matilde Sanchez-Pena, Juan Ortega-Alvarez, Genisson Coutinho

[2016]

↓ Outstanding Alumni and Student Honorees at the annual celebration dinner | LEFT TO RIGHT Natascha Trellinger, Schyler Curtice, Alex Klapka, Holly Simmons, Sonja Adams, Catherine Berdanier (Not Pictured: Lauren Denney and Sean Obrecht)

Allison Godwin
NSF CAREER

Holly Simmons
Outstanding Alumni Award

Phillip Wankat
Morrill Award

[2016]

CHAPTER 5
PEOPLE 1953–2016

This pictorial history is the story of the many people who have made unique contributions through their diverse skills, knowledge and abilities to the success of this School and its predecessors.

Over the past sixty years, first as the Department of Freshman Engineering, and the Division of Interdisciplinary Engineering Studies and now the School of Engineering Education, we have been served by a total of ten Heads, three of whom led two of these units at different times. Since 1995 we have been ably supported by a very active Industrial Advisory Council. In addition, an Academic Advisory Council, comprised of leading educators nationally, provided guidance during the formative years of the School of Engineering Education.

Commencing 1999, we have recognized graduates from the Interdisciplinary Engineering Studies program who have made outstanding contributions in their respective field. Four of these were subsequently recognized as Distinguished Engineering Alumni by the College of Engineering. From 2009, our Outstanding Alumni and Alumnae Awards have been open to graduates from all the degree programs in Engineering Education.

We have attracted a critical mass of nationally and internationally recognized faculty members. The work of these eminent scholars helps guide how Purdue and other institutions engage and educate engineering learners across a lifetime. From their home in the School of Engineering Education, our faculty are prominent and influential thought leaders in the national discourse on engineering education.

From a founding core of six faculty members in 2004, this number has more than quadrupled, bringing together a diverse mix of scholars from around the world. We are proud that half our faculty are women, reflecting the future composition of the profession. Thus far, an unprecedented total of thirteen current or former faculty in the School have received a prestigious NSF-CAREER award; four of these were subsequently awarded a Presidential Early Career Award for Scientists and Engineers.

Accomplishing the mission of the school critically depends upon a talented cadre of staff. Teaching and research are supported by a wide variety of professionals. Our dedicated Academic Advisors guide 2500 First-Year Engineering students annually as they navigate the transition from high school to college. In addition, undergraduates in Multidisciplinary Engineering and Interdisciplinary Engineering Studies are advised on their many options, including designing their own unique plan of study.

The Assistant Head for First-Year provides overall leadership for the strategic direction of that program while the Instructional Support Team work closely with our faculty and other instructional staff to co-design, support and deliver the learning experience of our First-Year Engineering students. The Director of Communication and the Director of Development work closely with the Head to engage the many external stakeholders of the School. Administrative assistants and clerical staff help to make the whole operation run smoothly.

Faculty and staff participating in a discussion during the 2014 ENE Advance

Engineering Education Heads

Department of Freshman Engineering (1954-2004)

Albert Spalding (Founding Head) 1953-1967
Clifford Gerde 1967-1973
Harold Amrine 1973-1981
Richard Grace 1981-1987
Phillip Wankat 1987-1995
Victor Goldschmidt 1996-2000
Jennifer Sinclair Curtis 2000-2003
Kamyar Haghighi 2003-2004

Division of Interdisciplinary Engineering Studies (1969-2004)

Richard Grace (Founding Head)....................1969-1982
David Kessler 1982-2000
Phillip Wankat 2000-2004

School of Engineering Education (2004-2016)

Kamyar Haghighi (Founding Head) 2004-2009
David Radcliffe (Interim Head) 2009-2010
David Radcliffe (Kamyar Haghighi Head) 2010-2016

Albert Spaulding

Clifford Gerde

Harold Amrine

Richard Grace

Phillip Wankat

David Kessler

Victor Goldschmidt

Jennifer Sinclair Curtis

Kamyar Haghighi

David Radcliffe

Advisory Councils

Engineering Education Industrial Advisory Council Members (2004-2016)

Rob Baird
General Motors

David Berlien
DuPont

Dianne Beever
Independent Consultant

Krista Comstock
The Proctor and Gamble Company

Gary Cummings
GM Corporation

Isadore Davis
Rolls-Royce Corporation

Robert Davis
Air Products (Chair 2004-2007)

Bud DeCoste
Schlumber

Jeff Detrick
GE Corporation

Sara D.B. Evans
Exxon Mobil

Dan Fillenwarth
Praxair Surface Technologies

Norman L. Fortenberry
National Academy of Engineering

Patricia D. Galloway
Nielsen-Wuster Group, Inc

Brian Gilmore
Deere and Company

Phillip C. Gould
Lockheed Martin

Lisa A. Hanson
Delphi Corporation

Gary Hobbs
Roch Diagnostics

Lila Ibrahim
Intel Corporation

Dick Ifkovits
Whirlpool Corporation

Timothy L. Jacobs
US Airways

Shari Kennet
Dow Chemical Company

Rick Kosdrosky
BAE Systems, Inc.

Candee Krautkramer
Kimberly-Clark Corporation

Thomas J. Lange
Procter & Gamble Company

Larry Leising
Schlumberger

Christine Maziar
University of Notre Dame

Reginald McGregor
Rolls-Royce North American

Tim Moser
Praxair

Bill Muzzillo
General Motors

Judy A. Nottoli
MWH Americas, Inc

Hugo Poza
Raytheon

Michael Pfeiffer
Eli Lilly and Company

Chris Rehrig
Air Products and Chemicals, Inc.

Mary Smith
Walker Parking Consultants

Brian Stutts
Corning Incorporated

Ellen E. Tobias
Eli Lilly and Company

Rick Zadoks
Caterpillar, Inc. (Chair 2010-2015)

Adel Zakaria
Deere & Company

Tom Zimmerman
Schlumberger (Chair 2007-2010)

Between 1995 and 2004, the Freshman Engineering Industry Advisory Council served a similar function. A number the people served on both Councils.

Engineering Education Academic Advisory Council Members (2005-2010)

Dr. Jim Pellegrino (Chair)
University of Illinois at Chicago

Dr. Dick Benson
Virginia Tech

Dr. Daryl E. Chubin
AAAS

Dr. Margaret Eisenhart
University of Colorado at Boulder

Dr. Richard M. Felder
North Carolina State University

Dr. Norman L. Fortenberry
CASEE

Dr. Linda Katehi
University of California, Davis

Dr. Jack R. Lohmann
Georgia Institute of Technology

Dr. Wendy Newstetter
Georgia Institute of Technology

Dr. Barbara M. Olds
Colorado School of Mines

Dr. Keith Sawyer
Washington University in St. Louis

Dr. Sheri Sheppard
Stanford University

Outstanding Alumni and Alumnae

Gregory Ayers
1999

Paul Cloyd
2001

Sue Hudson Abreu
2001

Michael Cave
2002

David Schwind
2002

Geoffrey Crowley
2003

Harold Aberman
2009

Brian Farley
2009

Gary Horlacher
2009

Robert Sharpe, Jr.
2009

Mary Spiess Smith
2009

Howard Gobstein
2010

Debra Echt
2011

Raymond Klein
2011

Richard Le Sesne
2011

Leslie Bottorff
2012

Rick Kosdrosky
2012

Stan Jones
2013

Eric Schmidt
2013

Michael Wells
2013

Rex Carter
2014

Henry Frissora
2015

Holly Simmons
2016

Distinguished Engineering Alumni

2001 .... **Gregory Martin Ayers**
2008 .... **Mike Cave**
2010 .... **Geoffrey T. Crowley**
2011 .... **David Schwind**

ENGINEERING
EDUCATION
OUTSTANDING
ALUMNI
AWARDS

EAST-WEST FACULTY LOUNGE ■ PURDUE MEMORIAL UNION
Purdue University

CHAPTER 5 FEATURE

CHALLENGES AND OPPORTUNITIES

Challenges From the outset it was recognized that creating an academic department where faculty undertook educational rather than traditional technical research brought with it both challenges and opportunities for prospective new hires joining a research intensive college like Purdue Engineering.

> *Engineering faculty's skepticism of engineering education as a scholarly activity has created an environment at many institutions that make the pursuit of deeply focused and productive engineering education research program anywhere from difficult to impossible. In some instances, engineering faculty with a high level of interest in engineering education carry above average teaching loads and are advised to develop and maintain traditional engineering research programs to ensure tenure. These faculty pursue engineering education projects as a sideline activity that often must be accomplished with little resources (e.g. time, funding, or graduate students). Alternatively, engineering faculty pursuing engineering education are relegated to non-tenure track positions even while they perform equivalent research activities (e.g. seeking and securing funding, conducting research, and presenting research results at professional conferences and publishing them in refereed journals).*
>
> Katehi, L.P.B., Banks, K., Diefes-Dux, H.A., Follman, D.K., Gaunt, J., Haghighi, K., Imbrie, P.K., Jamieson, L.H., Montgomery, R.E., Oakes, W.C. and Wankat, P. (2004) A New Framework for Academic Reform in Engineering Education, *Proceedings ASEE Annual Conference*, Salt Lake City, Session 2630.

The faculty of the School of Engineering Education, ably supported by dedicated staff, have risen to meet these challenges, and more. Like Dean Hawkins fifty years ago, they faced resistance but they pressed on to achieve great things. Now as the number of engineering education programs and departments grows nationally and globally, so a new set of challenges emerge with this evolving landscape, but nothing that is insurmountable.

↓↑ See pages for additional faculty and student activities: 52, 58, 107, 111, 112

Opportunities It was also clear from the beginning that the need for reform brought with it many exciting opportunities.

> *The call for engineering education reform on a number of fronts is driving the need for the establishment of the field of engineering education as a scholarly endeavor. This call for reform is exemplified in the 1994 joint project report on Engineering Education for a Changing World by the Engineering Deans Council and Corporate Roundtable of the American Society for Engineering Education, the 1995 Report by the Board on Engineering Education of the National Research Council, and the recent call for change by the National Academy of Engineering (NAE) leadership2-4. In addition, the adoption of ABET Engineering Criteria 2000 has intensified an interest in assessment of educational outcomes and promoted a recognition of the need for changes in pedagogy to achieve the varied outcomes.*
>
> *The National Science Foundation has supported educational scholarship in engineering since the late 1980's through the Division of Undergraduate Education and the Engineering Education Coalitions program. …Such support "has increased the status of educational research in faculty performance reviews, improved its quality by demanding appropriate assessment of results, attracted additional engineering professors into the arena, and increased collaborations between engineering professors and professors in disciplines like education and psychology.*
>
> Katehi, L.P.B., Banks, K., Diefes-Dux, H.A., Follman, D.K., Gaunt, J., Haghighi, K., Imbrie, P.K., Jamieson, L.H., Montgomery, R.E., Oakes, W.C. and Wankat, P. (2004) A New Framework for Academic Reform in Engineering Education, *Proceedings ASEE Annual Conference*, Salt Lake City, Session 2630.

Many of these opportunities have been grasped; new ones are before us as we continue into our second decade.

Faculty

Robin Adams
Associate Professor

Edward Berger
Associate Professor

Sean Brophy
Associate Professor

Monica Cardella
Associate Professor
Executive Director, Research Institute for Pre-College Engineering (INSPIRE)

Jennifer DeBoer
Assistant Professor

Heidi Diefes-Dux
Professor

Kerrie Anna Douglas
Visiting Assistant Professor

Audeen Fentiman
Crowley Family Professor of Engineering Education

Allison Godwin
Assistant Professor

Dale Harris
Executive Director, Engineering Professional Education

Morgan Hynes
Assistant Professor

Brent Jesiek
Associate Professor

Isabel Jimenez-Useche
Visiting Assistant Professor

Michael Loui
Dale and Suzi Gallagher Professor of Engineering Education

Krishna Madhaven
Associate Professor

Joyce Main
Assistant Professor

Muhsin Menekse
Assistant Professor

Tamera Moore
Associate Professor

William Oakes
Professor; Director of EPICS

Matthew Ohland
Professor

Alice Pawley
Associate Professor

Mary Pilotte
Associate Professor of Engineering Practice

Senay Purzer
Associate Professor

David Radcliffe
Kamyar Haghighi Head of the School of Engineering Education and Epistemology Professor of Engineering Education

Karl Smith
Cooperative Learning Professor

Ruth Streveler
Associate Professor

Phillip Wankat
Clifton L. Lovell Distinguished Professor of Chemical Engineering and Professor of Engineering Education

Courtesy Faculty

Gary Bertoline
Professor/Dean of the Purdue Polytechnic Institute

George Bodner
Professor/Arthur Kelly Distinguished Professor Chemical Education

Patrice Buzzanell
Professor, Brian Lamb School of Communication, School of Liberal Arts

Brenda Capobianco
Associate Professor/Science Education, Department of Curriculum & Instruction, COE

Nathalie Duval-Couetil
Associate Professor of Technology, Leadership, and Innovation

William Graziano
Professor/Department of Psychological Sciences

Leah Jamieson
Professor/Ransburg Professor of Electrical Computer Engineering/ John A. Edwardson Dean of Engineering

Alejandra Magana
Assistant Professor, Computer & Info Tech

Sharra Vostral
Associate Professor, Department of History

Staff

Sarah Allard
Academic Advisor

Dianne Bell
Administrative Assistant OPS Center

Carol Brock
Secretary

Lucero Campos
Business Manager

Anne DeLion
Instructional Support Coordinator

Jill Folkerts
Instructional Support Coordinator

Rebecca Fry
Director of Development

Elizabeth Gajdzik
Assistant Director, INSPIRE

Tamara Hare
Secretary V

Cindey Hays
Administrative Assistant
to the Head

Stephen Hoffmann
Assistant Head for
First-Year Engineering

Jeffrey Huddleston
Artisan and Fabrication Lab Supervisor

Billi Jennings
Director of
First-Year Engineering Advising

Russell Long
Director of Project Assessment

Loretta McKinnis
Secretary V

Janet Meek
Instructional Support Coordinator

Jeffrey Myers
Academic Advisor

Curt Oechsle
Academic Advisor

Christine Pekny
Interdisciplinary Engineering
Program Advisor

Carol Powell
Academic Advisor

Carlene Quirk
Secretary IV

Rose Redington
Academic Advisor

Julie Russell
Secretary V

Terri Sanger
Research Data and
Community Coordinator, INSPIRE

Laurie Snyder
Academic Advisor

Michele Strutz
Continuing Lecturer

Nathan Thomas
Senior Academic Advisor

Suzanne Coolbaugh-Walker
Academic Advisor

Teresa Walker
Director of Communications

James Whitford
Instructional Support Coordinator

Kathleen Wible
Continuing Term Lecturer

Richard Womack
Instructional Support Specialist

Kelly Wrede
Academic Advisor

PhD Graduates 2006–2016

Benjamin Ahn
2014

Aikaterini Bagiati
2011

Diana Bairaktarova
2013

Barry Brock
2009

Gregory Bucks
2010

Catherine Berdanier
2016

James Cawthorne
2016

Rocio Chavela Guerra
2011

Xin Chen
2015

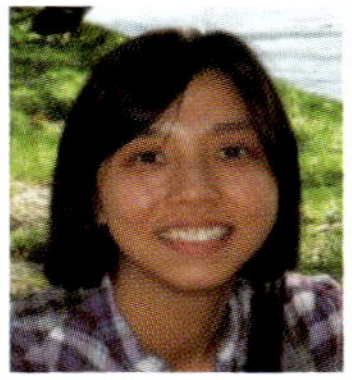
Xingyu Chen
2014

Tameka Clarke
2010

Antonette Cummings
2015

Odesma Dalrymple
2009

Shannon Daly
2007

Dana Denick
2015

Brianna Dorie
2015

Emily Dringenberg
2015

Farrah Fayyaz
2014

Daniel Ferguson
2013

Velvet Fitzpatrick
2014

Lorie Groll
2013

Justin Hess
2015

Elizabeth Holloway
2013

Ming-chien Hsu
2015

James Huff
2014

Mica Hutchinson-Green
2007

Qu Jin
2013

Shawn Jordan
2010

Sensen Li
2013

Jien-jou Lin
2013

Jeremi London
2013

Anne Lucietto
2014

Alejandra Magana de Leon
2009

Farshid Marbouti
2016

Holly Matusovich
2008

Jaqi McNeil
2014

Nathan McNeill
2010

Irene Mena
2010

Marisol Mercado
2014

Kerry Meyers
2009

Joi-lyn Mondisa
2015

Tamara Moore
2006

Ida Ngambeki
2012

Eurdice Oware
2008

Rui Pan
2014

Nataliia Perova
2015

Mary Pilotte
2013

Nicole Pitterson
2015

Kenneth Reed
2009

George Dante Ricco
2013

Kelsey Rogers
2016

Meagan Ross
2014

Anastastia Rynearson
2016

Lee Rynearson
2016

Noah Salzman
2012

Aidsa Santiago Roman
2009

Corey Schimpf
2015

Junaid Abdul Wahid Siddiqui 2014

Michele Strutz
2012

Marianna Tafur
2015

Julia Thompson
2015

Yogesh Venlankar
2010

Matthew Verleger
2009

Junqiu Wang
2014

Ruth Wertz
2014

Hanjun Xian
2013

Michele Yatchmeneff
2015

Jiabin Zhu
2013

Carla Zoltowski
2010

About the Author

Dr. Radcliffe received his B.S. and M.S. degrees in mechanical engineering from the University of Queensland, Australia and a Ph.D. in bioengineering from Strathclyde University in Scotland. He joined the Purdue in 2007 as the Epistemology Professor of Engineering Education. He was appointed as Associate Head of the School of Engineering Education in January 2009 and Interim Head from June 2009 to April 2010. In May 2010, he was appointed as the first Kamyar Haghighi Head of the School and served in that capacity until August 2016. Prior to joining Purdue he taught and conducted research at various universities in Australia, the UK and the US including the University of Queensland, Melbourne University, Adelaide University, Bath University and Stanford. Dr. Radcliffe is a Fellow, Institution of Engineers Australia, a Chartered Professional Engineer, a Fellow of the American Society of Engineering Education, a Fellow of European Society of Engineering Education, and a Past President of the Australasian Association for Engineering Education.

About the Designer and Book

Teresa Walker is a graduate from Saint Mary-of-the-Woods College with a degree in digital media communication and a 2016 graduate from the Brian Lamb School of Communication at Purdue University earning a master's degree in strategic communication. The book was a timely project, as she joined the School of Engineering Education in August of 2015—only a few months before the project began. It provided her a unique opportunity to learn in much detail the school history and the community that shaped what she is now supporting in her new role. Dr. Radcliffe's vision of the book, as it became affectionately called the "coffee table book or CTB," came to life through many drafts, planning meetings, transatlantic e-mails and cross country phone calls. The familiar faces and names threaded throughout the chapters and pages embrace the essence of Dr. Radcliffe's goal for the book—to articulate the many driving forces that shaped the School of Engineering Education and to celebrate the abundant successes of those who worked so hard over decades with dedication to engineering education.

Others Who Contributed

The staff in the Virginia Kelly Karnes Archives and Special Collections Research Center of the Purdue University Libraries were extremely helpful in sourcing original archival photos that led up to the formation of the School. Particularly, we would like to thank Neal Harmeyer, Digital Archivist, for going above and beyond in locating archived materials. These important resources helped reveal the journey of the outlined transitions and the stakeholders who blazed the trail. Also, a special thanks to Bryan Shaffer of the Purdue University Press for his wisdom and guiding hand through the book publishing process. Many members of the School contributed historical artifacts and pictures to be included and helped to identify people in the pictures, especially those from the early days. Robin Adams provided insightful feedback and helpful suggestions during the formative stages development of the book.

Additional Photo Contributors
Caleb Carithers
Suzanne Coolbaugh-Walker
Rebecca Fry
Purdue University
Alice Pawley
David Radcliffe
Karl Smith
Teresa Walker
The White House